VISUAL MUSIC

Interpreting Songs in
American Sign Language

Rev. Dr. Raymont L. Anderson

authorHOUSE®

AuthorHouse™
1663 Liberty Drive
Bloomington, IN 47403
www.authorhouse.com
Phone: 1-800-839-8640

First published by AuthorHouse 12/18/2009

ISBN: 978-1-4343-7252-9 (sc)

Library of Congress Control Number: 2009911376

Printed in the United States of America
Bloomington, Indiana

This book is printed on acid-free paper.

TABLE OF CONTENTS

DEDICATION / ACKNOWLEDGEMENTS

To all of those that inspired, supported, guided, instructed, listened, and pushed!

To my parents – Lois and Charles Anderson for encouraging me, caring for me, and letting me grow and explore life in my search for self. To my brothers and family who have supported and encouraged me along the way. To my son Kenneth Grimmett III for being a continued source of strength, inspiration, and love.

To my friends Sensei Ruriko Masutani, Sylvia Love, Charlsia Fortner, Tracy Rhymes, James Miller, Ernest Garrett III, Eamonn Knight, Ann Sun, and Nino for being "family" to me.

To my ASL people – Linda Bove, for being my first source of ASL inspiration when I saw her on Sesame Street and for her encouragement when I met her during the run of Big River in both NYC and DC; to Karen McGann, my first official ASL teacher, for encouraging me to use ASL to perform and encouraging me to continue when I wanted to stop; to Nancy DeWitt for helping me be comfortable with who I am; and to Dr. Brian Cerney, for being one of my most direct and helpful mentors, for helping me become not only a more proficient interpreter but an ASLTA certified ASL teacher and a much more skilled ASL performer as well.

To my Theatre people – Dr. Noreen Barnes-McLean, my mentor and advisor who believed in me as I took a leap of faith into the land of Theatre Pedagogy; Gary Hooper for taking a risk and casting me in "The Day the Bronx Died," an experience that changed my life, David Leong for accepting nothing less than excellence, and the late Marvin Simms who not only reminded me that it was ok to grieve my father's passing but that grieving did not mean forgetting. Marvin also taught me not to accept anything less than the best of myself.

To those whom I have yet to meet but who have inspired me as well: Oprah Winfrey, Dr. Wayne Dyer, Farah Gray, Marianne Williamson, James Arthur Ray, Jack Canefiled, Robin Williams, Christopher Reeve, Rhonda Britten, Iyanla Vanzant and more. I thank them for being who they are, for showing me that I did not have to continue to live in the darkness, and not only could I live in the light, but, share the light that is within me.

Special thanks for their assistance and feedback – Leo Yates Jr., author of "Interpreting at Church: A Paradigm for Sign Language Interpreters," Dr. Bill Vicars of ASL University, and my editors: Brittany Love, Terrye Hicks, and Tracy Rhymes.

And most importantly, to God, the great Divine Spirit for being the supportive loving power that gives me life, breath, and the love and inspiration to do as Gandhi did, "To be the change."

PREFACE

Over the last hundred years, the method used by deaf people to communicate has gone through a variety of changes, as have the names hearing people have given to deaf people. From being considered merely a form of gestures used by "deaf and dumb" to a form of English on the hands used by "deaf mutes" to what it really is: a complete language used by Deaf people with their own culture and community – American Sign Language (ASL). As ASL evolved and became more accessible (via more formal education) to more people, both Deaf and hearing, it also opened the doors for new professions (sign language interpreters, ASL teachers, teachers of the deaf) and new forms of creative expression (theaters for the Deaf, ASL choirs, and ASL poetry). It is the performing art aspect of ASL, specifically the signing of songs (interpreting songs and performing), that I will focus on.

This text will be of benefit to anyone seeking to learn more about the art of interpreting songs, performing songs, working with glosses and translating from English to ASL. Actually, this text will benefit anyone studying ASL, as I will talk a lot about conceptual meanings versus literal or word-based meaning. For example, there is not a specific sign for "nightmare" so conceptually you must sign something like "bad+dream." Another example is the following sentence: *Law and Order* is my favorite TV show." Where "TV show" would be signed, "TV+show." The sign for "show" would be done as "drama/act", or "program" and not "show" meaning demonstrate or example.

Anyone seeking to have a stronger grasp of conceptual meanings can benefit from this text as I have created it. It is my hope that the easy reading format and the repetition of key themes are of great benefit to you. You will also have several chapters that cover various topics, so everyone can find material of benefit to them.

INTRODUCTION

Over the years, I have met countless people who desire to sign (interpret or perform) songs in ASL. It has been my experience that, of those that want to do this, many are unaware of how to do so in a conceptually accurate manner. There are many people stuck in the box of transliteration only because they don't know how to get out of that particular box. Many of us are not taught how to sign in a more idiomatic and visual manner, let alone sign songs that are inherently more conceptual than literal.

What I am presenting for you in this text is a summarized version of what I teach in my "American Sign Language and Performing" class at Prince George's Community College. I have selected several of the tools and skills that I have learned and have used since beginning this performance art form in 1992. Having successfully used them and taught them to others who have also successfully used, I know that they work. My presentation format is similar to the way I teach the course and I hope that you find it as easy to follow and free flowing as you would in the class.

While this book was written to address certain issues related to "perform / interpret" songs in ASL, I want to make sure it is clear that this text is also of benefit to those who adamantly are opposed and disinterested with music and ASL. The skills I will introduce, such as conceptual accuracy, use of facial expression and body language as a storytelling device, use of visual vernacular, acting and several "Rayisms," will be beneficial to anyone and everyone seeking to improve their expressive ASL skills.

OK, so relax, take a breath, turn the pages, and get ready to put your hands up and sign, act, and dance your way to greater proficiency.

THE BASICS: INTERPRETING

While this book is not *solely* about interpreting, remember that it IS about interpreting. It is ALSO about translating. It is ALSO about performing. This book is about many things. Because all of them are interrelated, it is my intention that this text will help you to develop skills in each of these areas, but more importantly, your ASL skills overall. The following terms may at first seem to apply to those of us who work as interpreters and those aspiring to be interpreters, it is also important for non-interpreters to remember certain vocabulary, as well as a few of the Do's and Don'ts of interpreting because much of what will be discussed will apply to non-interpreters as well.

Vocabulary
- Interpret / Transliterate
- Simultaneous interpreting / Consecutive interpreting
- Translating
- Unduly free and imposed meaning
- Text- Source language, Frozen Text
- Target- Target language (ASL), Gloss
- Team- People involved in the project
- Tools- All materials used to assist in translation (dictionaries, etc.)
- Gender specificity
- Implicit / Explicit meanings

Interpret / Transliterate

"Interpreting is the process of <u>understanding</u> (or <u>comprehending</u>) a message in one language and then <u>creating</u> (or <u>generating</u>) it in another." It is important to understand that transliterating which is also literal interpreting / literal translating is not the same as idiomatic interpreting / idiomatic translating. Literal translations or interpretations are defined as being a word-for-word / meaning-for-meaning process (see Japanese example). Incorrect conceptual matching is not actually a goal for any professional interpreter or translator (although it is a goal for some comedians). So if people mismatch their concepts, then they are just not doing a good job.

Literal interpreting would get the correct concepts lined up in the same order as the source text (usually in conflict with natural idiomatic syntax and discourse). Idiomatic interpreting would have the correct concepts (although perhaps different vocabulary choices than the literal version) arranged in a way so that the result looks natural, not like an interpretation, but more like a text originally created in the target language.

Japanese example of literal translation: Taking the Japanese kanji 愛 which when presented in a literal translation into English is Ai. When translated idiomatically you are given the meaning – Love.

In terms of ASL and English, an example would be using fingerspelling or mouth movements without any ASL signs.

As interpreters, when you are on the job, you must ask what does the client want you to provide. Does he/she want more idiomatic interpreting or literal interpreting? You then give the client what they prefer. Because this book is targeting skill development, I am focusing more on the idiomatic translation / idiomatic interpreting skill. I want us to develop the skill of making the English text (spoken, sung) a visually pleasing, conceptually accurate, and idiomatically translated product.

Simultaneous interpreting / Consecutive interpreting

"Simultaneous interpreting occurs when the interpreter generates a target text while the source text is still being produced. The interpreter has little processing time to comprehend the source and regenerate it in the target language. This overlap of source and target texts reduces the interpreter's ability to generate the target text in a conceptually correct (and idiomatic) manner."

"Consecutive interpreting occurs when the interpreter generates a target text in between segments of the source text. This means that the interpreter has processing time, without overlapping, to first listen to the source text, process it, and then produce the target language."

By improving your ability to take the needed time to process the information, you more accurately create a product that the deaf person can clearly understand. The full meaning of what is being said is now effectively conveyed rather than the deaf person having to piece strings of thoughts or words together to figure out the message. The more completely *you* understand the message, the more effectively you can render that message visually and conceptually in the target language.

TRANSLATING

"Translation occurs when the interpreter/translator generates a target text after the entire source text has been completed." Here is an example: Suppose you have the Lord's Prayer in English as your frozen text (which is text that does not change; it remains the same each time it is said), after reading it through line by line, you produce an idiomatic translation of that text. You would then do a performed translation of the text when someone verbally presents the prayer. Many interpreters benefit from performed translations with texts like the Pledge of Allegiance, Lord's Prayer, Doxology, the Miranda Warning and the National Anthem, for example. It becomes much easier to do your job when you already have a familiar translation of the text. For one thing, you do not have to process the information you hear as if for the first time; you already know the text and therefore are more likely to produce an accurate interpretation.

I suggest that if you are a religious interpreter, aspiring interpreter or working interpreter who has not considered doing so, begin to create a translation of the texts you frequently encounter. If you do a particular church service, create a frozen text of the texts repeated weekly. If you interpret in an educational setting and the Pledge of Allegiance is recited, create a frozen text of it; same thing for the school alma mater and any other texts that you encounter frequently.

Unduly Free and Imposed Meaning

The job of an interpreter is to make sure the target language retains the meaning of the source, i.e., if someone signs something (source language), then you must voice it (target language) in a manner that is accurate to what the deaf person intended and vice versa. If you are hearing spoken English (source) and you are signing it (target), your interpretation must be true to the speaker's intent and meaning. You must be careful not to alter the meaning of the source due to a mistake in understanding or even worse – deliberately. Suppose you are interpreting at an event and the speaker says something you personally do not agree with: for example abortion, war, gay marriage, legalizing drugs. Do you interpret what the speaker says despite your personal feelings or do you alter the meaning to fit your personal ideologies? If you change the message, you are being unduly free in your interpretation of the material and that is against the professional code of ethics, FYI!

There are some instances where you may not know the meaning, this happens frequently with poetry readings, songs, or some speeches where the person takes several tangents that are hard to follow. Your task is to do the best you can do with what you have. The main warning with being unduly free is in imposing your select meaning on it when you know or are reasonably certain that it is incorrect.

"I don't want to go to school today." - Does not equate with - "I am not going to school today."

As I mentioned a moment ago, when doing music and poetry, you often do not have the luxury of having the source's meaning be that clear. In order to sign something, you the interpreter must know what it means or have some idea. Even if you choose to fingerspell it, a degree of understanding is necessary or confusion may ensue. For example, you are interpreting in a government setting that uses acronyms and they say what sounds like FURS which is actually spelled FERS or sounds like "FACTS" versus "FAQS." Many acronyms are not spelled out like N.A.D. or U.S.D.A. they are said as a word like NASA or NOAA (which is pronounced Noah). If fingerspelled without knowing the actual use and spelling, the true meaning can easily become misrepresented.

You will, at times, have to make choices based upon what you think something means and then later may realize you were off track. That is part of the job. However, when you either knowingly apply a meaning that is not true to the source or you do not take the time to be responsible and research appropriate meaning, you are doing a huge misrepresentation to the job, the client, the speaker, and yourself.

Let's look at an example:

Example One:
"GIRLS WANNA HAVE FUN" – Cyndi Lauper
The line in English says, "Girls just wanna have fun"
Suppose the interpreter took that line of the text and signed in a way that meant:
"Girls want to have sex, do drugs, party and go wild!"

Does that retain the meaning of the source or is it unduly free?
Clearly it is unduly free.

Example Two:
Genesis 2:
16 And the LORD God commanded the man, saying, of every tree of the garden thou mayest freely eat:
17 But of the tree of the knowledge of good and evil, thou shalt not eat of it: for in the day that thou eatest thereof thou shalt surely die.

Suppose the interpreter took that line of the text and signed in a way that meant:
"If you eat from that tree I'll kill you!"

Does that retain the meaning of the source or is it unduly free?

Text – Source Language, Frozen Text

Source Language is the language you are starting with; the language you are interpreting from. For interpreters the source is English in which case the target is then ASL or vice versa – the source is ASL and the target is spoken (voiced) English.

Frozen text is text that does not change; it remains the same each time it is said. Most often, interpreters do not have an actual text to work from. However, in certain circumstances, you do. As performers you always have the ability to do a performed translation. A performed translation is similar to frozen text. Having had time to translate, rehearse, and memorize the translation, you can do the same signs each time you do the text. For example, in church settings you would do a performed translation of the Lord's Prayer each time it is sung during service.

Benefits of having the text and doing a performed translation from that text include:

- Time to work through and research meaning of the text,
- Time to work out a conceptually accurate way to sign it,
- Each time you encounter that text you already have the translation in your bag of tricks.

Not all frozen source materials are actual texts on paper, some are spoken "texts" that are nonetheless frozen (unchanging): The Miranda Warning, the Lord's Prayer, and The Pledge of Allegiance, for example, are spoken source material "texts" that are frozen and can be done as performed translations.

You have various texts that you will be working from at various times, so it is in your best interest to take time in advance to study the source text and think about how you could translate it and thus interpret it.

Clearly, when you are working from a text, getting it in advance and becoming familiar with it so you competently interpret the material in the target language is the most efficient and professional thing to do.

Look at the following three examples of texts that interpreters have interpreted at some point or another. I found them to be of great value to certified and uncertified interpreters as exercises or lessons in conceptualizing. Pay special attention to the words and phrases that you find difficult or interesting and those that could present a particular challenge for you, thinking about how you would "Put that on your hands," meaning how would you sign it.

"Lift Every Voice and Sing" also known as -
"The Negro National Anthem"
by James Weldon Johnson

Lift every voice and sing
Till earth and heaven ring,
Ring with the harmonies of Liberty;
Let our rejoicing rise
High as the listening skies,
Let it resound loud as the rolling sea.
Sing a song full of the faith that the dark past has taught us,
Sing a song full of the hope that the present has brought us,
Facing the rising sun of our new day begun
Let us march on till victory is won.

Stony the road we trod,
Bitter the chastening rod,
Felt in the days when hope unborn had died;
Yet with a steady beat,
Have not our weary feet
Come to the place for which our fathers sighed?
We have come over a way that with tears have been watered,
We have come, treading our path through the blood of the slaughtered,

Out from the gloomy past,
Till now we stand at last
Where the white gleam of our bright star is cast.

God of our weary years,
God of our silent tears,
Thou who has brought us thus far on the way;
Thou who has by Thy might
Led us into the light,
Keep us forever in the path, we pray.
Lest our feet stray from the places, Our God, where we met Thee;
Lest our hearts drunk with the wine of the world, we forget Thee;
Shadowed beneath Thy hand,
May we forever stand.
True to our GOD,
True to our native land

Pledge of Allegiance

I Pledge Allegiance to the flag of the United States of America and to
the Republic for which it stands, one Nation under God, indivisible,
with liberty and justice for all.

Star Spangled Banner

O say, can you see, by the dawn's early light,
What so proudly we hailed at the twilight's last gleaming,
Whose broad stripes and bright stars, through the perilous fight,
O'er the ramparts we watched, were so gallantly streaming?
And the rockets' red glare, the bombs bursting in air,
Gave proof through the night that our flag was still there;
O say, does that star-spangled banner yet wave
O'er the land of the free and the home of the brave?

On the shore, dimly seen thro' the mist of the deep,
Where the foe's haughty host in dread silence reposes,
What is that which the breeze, o'er the towering steep.
As it fitfully blows, half conceals, half discloses?

Now it catches the gleam of the morning's first beam,
In full glory reflected, now shines on the stream
'Tis the star-spangled banner. Oh! Long may it wave
O'er the land of the free and the home of the brave!

And where is that band who so vauntingly swore
That the havoc of war and the battle's confusion
A home and a country should leave us no more?
Their blood has washed out their foul footstep's pollution.
No refuge could save the hireling and slave

From the terror of flight, or the gloom of the grave,
And the star-spangled banner in triumph doth wave
O'er the land of the free and the home of the brave.

Oh! thus be it ever, when freemen shall stand
Between their loved homes and the war's desolation,
Blest with vict'ry and peace, may the Heav'n-rescued land
Praise the Pow'r that hath made and preserved us a nation!
Then conquer we must, when our cause it is just,
And this be our motto—"In God is our trust."
And the star-spangled banner in triumph shall wave
O'er the land of the free and the home of the brave.

In order to put any of these three examples on your hands, you would first need to know what it means, right? I have witnessed people attempt to sign the Star Spangled Banner who did not realize "Star Spangled Banner" means the U.S. Flag. What about "Rampart"? Do you know what it is, what it means, or how to sign it conceptually? Many people don't and the worst thing is that many do not take the time to study, investigate, or learn to do it more appropriately.

From the three text examples I have given, there are a myriad of possible interpretations that could be signed, based on the interpreter's or performer's understanding or "lack of" understanding of the text's meaning. Always do the pre-work studying you need to do in order to do the best job possible.

There is even more of a mystery when you begin to do artistic, poetic, symbolic, or vague texts. The more often you encounter art forms such as literature, songs, and poetry, the more you will find artistic interpretation challenges and for those religious interpreters – the bible is replete with poetry and symbolism.

Take this scenario as an example:
You are the interpreter of a college level literature class and the teacher decides to spend several weeks on author Lewis Carroll. During that time "Alice in Wonderland" and "The Jabberwocky" will be studied. Have you ever read or heard "The Jabberwocky?"
It is replete with nonsense words that you, the interpreter, would still need to put on your hands for the deaf client. Granted he or she can read it and you can direct them to read the book. However, suppose the teacher recites it before handing out the text. What do you do then?

I have been in classes (both as a student and as the interpreter) where the material was not in the book and the teacher did not provide handouts; instead the teacher recited the poem from memory!
Now what do you do?

"JABBERWOCKY"
By Lewis Carroll (published 1871)

'Twas brillig, and the slithy toves
Did gyre and gimble in the wabe:
All mimsy were the borogoves,
And the mome raths outgrabe.
"Beware the Jabberwock, my son!
The jaws that bite, the claws that catch!
Beware the Jubjub bird, and shun
The frumious Bandersnatch!"
He took his vorpal sword in hand:
Long time the manxome foe he sought—
So rested he by the Tumtum tree,
And stood awhile in thought.

And, as in uffish thought he stood,
The Jabberwock, with eyes of flame,
Came whiffling through the tulgey wood,
And burbled as it came!
One, two! One, two! And through and through
The vorpal blade went snicker-snack!
He left it dead, and with its head
He went galumphing back.

"And, hast thou slain the Jabberwock?
Come to my arms, my beamish boy!
O frabjous day! Callooh! Callay!"
He chortled in his joy.
'Twas brillig, and the slithy toves
Did gyre and gimble in the wabe:
All mimsy were the borogoves,
And the mome raths outgrabe.

    The English source text is rather challenging and at first glance you may assume that an ASL translation would be impossible. However, think again. The complexity of this poem did not stop Eric Malzkuhn, a Gallaudet student who, in 1939, created an original rendition of the poem. Later, in 1967, when the National Theater of the Deaf was founded and Eric Malzkuhn was involved, it was his "Jabberwocky" translation that was assigned to a young actor, Joe Velez to perform. I strongly encourage you to view both Joe Velez's and Lou Fant's performance of the poem. Not only for the beauty of the artistry, but for the study of how nonexistent/nonsensical words were signed / gestured and produced in a beautifully clear and effective manner.

Target – Target language (ASL), Gloss

Target language refers to the manner in which the client wants you to sign; a more transliterated English word order form or a more conceptual idiomatic visual ASL form. It would also include Manually Coded English but for this text that is not where we are focusing. The focus of this text is not even the transliterated form. I am focusing on the idiomatic form and the attempt to be both as visually pleasing and conceptually correct as possible. In order to accomplish that end, we must be aware of several ASL grammatical features at our disposal that often go unused in musical interpretations and performances. Let's look at four of them at this time.

Rhetorical Questions
Topicalization
WH-Questions (Who, What, When, Where, Why, Which, How)
Conditionals

A rhetorical question is basically a statement made in the form of a question. You are asking a question that you, the giver of the message, will answer as a way of focusing on the answer. For example:

MY NAME WHAT? RAY.

DIE THERE CROSS WHO? JESUS.

TOMORROW WE GO WHERE? DISNEY WORLD.

I LIVE WHERE? MARYLAND.

As you see, I am not asking the receiver of the message for an answer to my questions; rather I am emphasizing the answer by setting it up as a rhetorical question. It is also important to note that facially, you do not ask a rhetorical question as you would a WH-question. For a WH-question, your eyebrows are furrowed down (like a frown). However, for a rhetorical question, your eyebrows are up.

Topicalization is when you typically place the topic at the beginning of the sentence. Again you raise your eyebrows when you sign the topic. For example:

FRIEND I SEE FINISH.

BOOK I READ WANT.

BICYCLE I BUY WILL.

THAT DVD I WANT.

WH-Questions are information – seeking questions where you ask who, what, when, where, why, which, or how. Remember that for WH-Questions you furrow your brows and slightly tilt your head leaning forward. For example:

YOUR NAME WHAT?

MY CLASSROOM WHERE?

HIS WIFE WHO?

OUR MEETING WHEN?

There is also an interesting thing that I find occurs with beginning and intermediate students, and that is their "word obsession." What I mean by that is when the person is seeking a specific sign to match for every word. There are times in ASL, as with all languages, when you will not have a word you can translate with an equivalent word. What do you do when you are faced with such a situation? First, I know many students respond by saying, "Look for the word," at which time they hunt through the dictionary or Internet for that word. However, there are, as I said, times when there is NO equivalent. Let's use the word *ninja,* for example. What is the sign for ninja? Whether there is one or not, let's – for the sake of conversation – say that there is none. It is common in ASL to refer to the word and explain a little about it. This even occurs at times when there IS a sign for a word but the person is emphasizing their point and making certain it is clear.

Let's use *ninja* as our first example. A ninja (in case you do not know) is a Japanese warrior of feudal Japan. They are often set as the antithesis of the Samurai. The ninja is typically characterized as the all black clad sword – toting assassin. Ok, now knowing that, you would be able to set up a sentence.

Example One:
Ray: LAST WEEK MOVIE "LAST SAMURAI" I SEE. GOOD MOVIE. I ENJOY. MOVIE HAVE N-I-N-J-A, I LIKE.

Sylvia: N-I-N-J-A?

Ray: YOU KNOW, SAME-AS SAMURAI BUT DRESS ALL BLACK, HIDE, FIGHT, SWORD on back.

Sylvia: OH-I-SEE

Example Two:
Ray: I WANT SEE MOVIE "PASSION OF THE CHRIST"

Margo: Puzzled look

Ray: KNOW, MOVIE ABOUT JESUS?

Margo: Still puzzled

Ray: KNOW STORY ABOUT J-E-S-U-S JESUS? JESUS CROSS CRUCIFY DIE, THAT JESUS. MOVIE THAT, JESUS, I WANT SEE!

Notice that in the second example, Ray fingerspells "Jesus" then signs it to clarify to Margo who he is talking about. Ray then gives a brief description that he believes Margo would understand about what happened to Jesus so that he can help her to understand what he is telling her about the movie.

I strongly encourage you to train yourself to think conceptually versus literally. Look at the following words; whether you know a sign for the word or not, for the sake of the exercise, imagine that there is no sign for the word. Also many times the person may not know the sign you are using. In these cases, how would you explain the concept?

- x Dinosaur
- x Dolphin
- x Mummy (as in Egyptian)
- x Transformer (the robots that change into vehicles)
- x God
- x Mother
- x Sister or Brother
- x President of the USA
- x Money
- x Seaweed
- x Philosophy
- x Stereotypes

Conditionals are the If / Then statements in ASL. *If* I go to the store, *then* I will buy the new Ipod. One thing happening is dependent upon the other thing. *If* it rains, *then* I will stay home. Conditionals have two parts – the condition and the consequence. With a conditional, you raise your eyebrows during the condition and lower them during the consequence. There are times when the signs #IF (*Note: # means to fingerspell*) or SUPPOSE may precede the condition. For example:

SUPPOSE MOM ARRIVE HOME LATE, GO GRANDMA HOUSE.

During the beginning portion of the sentence – SUPPOSE MOM ARRIVE HOME LATE – your eyebrows are raised.

During the second half – GO GRANDMA HOUSE – your eyebrows are lowered.

More examples of conditionals:

YOU USE MICROWAVE, YOU CLEAN.

IF WE GO MOVIES, YOU PAY.

I VISIT YOU RICHMOND, STAY YOUR HOUSE NOT HOTEL.

IF I SIT BACK – SEAT, VOMIT WILL.

There are several sentence structure types that occur in ASL that are of significant benefit to us as musical performers. I have given you a sampling of some of the easiest to begin incorporating into your daily conversation. Incorporating them into your musical interpreting will be of tremendous benefit as well.

When I teach workshops or ASL classes, students or participants often ask what a "gloss" is. To help those of you who may want to know, I am including it here as well. For those that already know, come along for the ride. Essentially a gloss is a place – holder that helps you to identify / remember a sign by using an English word. Glossing typically uses ALL CAPS to identify it as a gloss (place –holder) and not as an English word. Typically, fingerspelling is identified with dashes: R-A-Y-M-O-N-T A-N-D-E-R-S-O-N. Lexicalized fingerspelling is typically identified with a pound symbol in front such as #ALL versus ALL, #TV, #NO, #JOB, #IF, etc. Glosses generally don't identify tense or other English differences: SEE instead of SAW, CHANGE instead of CHANGED, I for the "I" handshape, ME for index-finger pointing. I tend to use the "first-person-pronoun" (1PP) so that my glosses don't read like a kind of broken English or what some may call Tarzan-speak—though there are times when my linguistic descriptions are not that detailed and specific.

The gloss would assist you in knowing what signs you may use when you have to interpret or when you do performed translation (which is when you have the text, and the sign choices set, so you would sign it the same each time you do it.) That is what I observed in many Deaf congregations where they sign the Lord's Prayer during service. Each service, the prayer is signed the same way and, therefore, is a performed translation not an interpretation. An example of an interpretation would be what I see in many hearing churches (with several interpreters)—where each interpreter has his/her own way of the signing the prayer.

Here is an example of a Gloss.

A- More literally translated Gloss:

English: For most of my elementary school years, I was frequently bullied. I had asked each of my five brothers, at some point, to teach me to fight but none of them ever did. Then one day, one of them took me to see a Bruce Lee double feature. From the moment I saw Bruce in action, I was committed to learning martial arts. Once I began studying, the bullying stopped. I went on to become a teacher and a continued fan of martial arts films.

Gloss: FOR MOST MY ELEMENTARY SCHOOL YEARS I OFTEN PICK-ON, BEAT-UP. I ASK EACH MY 5 BROTHER TEACH ME HOW FIGHT BUT NONE E-V-E-R DO. THEN ONE DAY, 1 BROTHER TAKE-ME SEE 2 B-R-U-C-E L-E-E MOVIE. FROM MOMENT WHEN I SEE B-R-U-C-E IN ACTION, I COMMIT LEARN M-A-R-T-I-A-L A-R-T-S. WHEN I BEGIN STUDY, PICK-ON, BEAT-UP STOP. I LATER BECAME TEACHER AND CONTINUE F-A-N M-A-R-T-I-A-L A-R-T MOVIE

English: For most of my elementary school years, I was frequently bullied. I had asked each of my five brothers, at some point, to teach me to fight but none of them ever did. Then one day, one of them took me to see a Bruce Lee double feature. From the moment I saw Bruce in action, I was committed to learning martial arts. Once I began studying, the bullying stopped. I went on to become a teacher and a continued fan of martial arts films.

Gloss: LONG-AGO HAPPEN I YOUNG, KNOW SCHOOL ELEMENTARY HAPPEN PEOPLE CL:1 come up to me PICK-ON, HIT-ME, TELL-ME MONEY GIVE-THEM. ANYWAY, THAT I FED-UP. HAVE 5 BROTHER ME. I ASK THEM WHAT? TEACH ME BOXING. I WAIT+++ THEY TEACH ME? NEVER HAPPEN. LATER, 1 BROTHER, ME, TWO-US GO MOVIE. SEE WHAT? B-R-U-C-E L-E-E MOVIE, 2.

HAPPEN I WATCH-MOVIE STRIKE-CHANCE DECIDE THAT KARATE, I LEARN WILL. LATER, I START STUDY, PRACTICE KARATE CALLED K-U-N-G F-U. CONTINUE, HAPPEN LATER TEACHER ME ALSO STILL F-A-N KARATE MOVIE I FASCINATE CRAZY-FOR!

The gloss can also include classifier use, mouthing morphemes, body language – whatever will assist you in remembering how to sign the text.

Gloss including some additional info: LONG-AGO HAPPEN I YOUNG, KNOW SCHOOL ELEMENTARY HAPPEN PEOPLE CL:1 come up to me PICK-ON, HIT-ME, TELL-ME MONEY GIVE-THEM (gesture digging in pockets to give money.) ANYWAY, THAT I FED-UP. HAVE 5 BROTHER ME. I ASK THEM WHAT? TEACH ME BOXING. I WAIT+++ THEY TEACH ME? NEVER

HAPPEN. LATER, 1 BROTHER, ME, TWO-US GO MOVIE. SEE WHAT? B-R-U-C-E L-E-E MOVIE, 2.

HAPPEN CL:11 (diagramming the huge screen, CHA mouthing morpheme) I WATCH-MOVIE STRIKE-CHANCE (POW mouthing morpheme) DECIDE THAT KARATE, I LEARN WILL. LATER, I START STUDY, PRACTICE (motorlips mouthing morpheme) KARATE CALLED K-U-N-G F-U. CONTINUE, HAPPEN TEACHER ME (PAH mouthing morpheme) ALSO STILL F-A-N KARATE MOVIE I FASCINATE CRAZY-FOR!

Team — People involved in the project

Team refers to the people you are working with. Many interpreters are increasingly getting to experience the benefits of team interpreting as the field continues to develop and grow. However, the team I am speaking of is not just the co-interpreter you work with. Depending on what you are interpreting (a theater production, rally at the Senate, Black History month assembly, a doctor appointment) your team consists of all the people involved in assisting you facilitate communication to the client.

The doctor becomes part of your team as you and she coordinate to facilitate the deaf patient's care. If the doctor says something that you are not sure of, in order to put it in ASL, you must know what it is or at least how to spell it, so you ask. Suppose the director of a play changes a line in the script—you must be made aware of such a change. Yet, the new line's meaning is unclear (maybe a character refers to "him" but you have no idea who that character is referring to.) In order to be clear in the interpretation of the play, you ask the director, an actor, or other knowledgeable person.

Anyone who can be of assistance to you in your facilitation of language to the deaf consumer is a part of your team. Since I mentioned it and I know many people who desire to interpret in a theatrical setting, let me expand upon the interpreting of a play a little more.

A play that is going to be interpreted has a team that consists of the Sign master, also called a Sign coach, or ASL coach (this position is usually held by a deaf professional who is well versed in theatre. This person may translate the entire play or oversee the interpreter to make sure the signs used for the play will be conceptually correct, accurate to the play, and clear), the interpreters, director and / or dramaturg (the one who does research for the production) for the play. Even the actors can offer particular insight into the text and / or delivery of the text. All of them become part of your team. And truth be told, the lighting designers who make sure you can be seen are part of your team as well.

If you are a religious interpreter, your team can include the pastor, minister of music, deacons, choir, and – as you will find – anyone who can assist you in your interpreting ministry during service.

Who is your team when you are working alone? Suppose you are asked to interpret or perform a song in ASL at a cousin's wedding, a retirement party, or a concert at a deaf camp. Who does your team consist of now? Your team now consists of all the tools you have at your disposal.

TOOLS – ALL MATERIALS USED
TO ASSIST IN TRANSLATION

A tool is anything you can potentially use that will help give insight, understanding, and clarity to the text so that you can create a translation.

Dictionaries, internet websites, text books, scripts, CD inserts with lyrics, Spark Notes, Magazine articles, and encyclopedias are all examples of tools that are available to you; and whether you are working alone or with your "team," they (your tools) also become part of your team.

Do not limit yourself; there is nearly an unlimited amount of resources and information available to us. If you need to call or visit the library or local university to speak to someone in a particular department, then do it. If you have a question, someone somewhere has an answer; find it.

GENDER SPECIFICITY

Gender specificity is matching male speaker (or client) to male interpreter or female to female. Many times in the field of interpreting, we are asked to match gender, especially for such things as medical appointments. However, there are other times where gender specificity is not an issue. Even when doing performed translations (which I will speak more about later), you the interpreter/performer can very well be a male while signing to a female vocalist and it is not an issue. Yet, there are certain songs where a male signing may look odd and could be potentially distracting. For example, signing to lyrics like Whitney Houston's "I'm Every Woman,": *I'm every woman, It's all in me.*

Make sure that you are aware of the song by doing your prep work, to know if gender will be of significance.

There are also times when a vague pronoun such as "she" might be uttered in the song. You would need to have a little more information in order to effectively put that on your hands.

For example:
"She went to the store."

How do you sign that?
How do you establish the female pronoun?

Possible solutions:
"WOMAN INDEX GO FINISH STORE"
"S-H-E INDEX GO FINISH STORE"

My point in stating what might seem obvious to some of you is that I have seen many situations where people simply pointed, INDEX the pronoun.

"INDEX GO FINISH STORE"

Without giving a gender, that sentence could be he or she. It needs to be set up in a more effective manner in order to make sense.

In the song, "I will follow Him" we find a similar issue where the masculine pronoun "he / him" is used to describe this person that the singer will follow.

"I WILL FOLLOW HIM"
Little Peggy March

I will follow Him (follow Him), Follow Him wherever He may go,
There isn't an ocean too deep, A mountain so high, it can keep,
Keep me away, away from His love

The song does not specifically identify who "he" is. We are left to infer possible details such as he is a boyfriend, someone she has a crush on, maybe a husband, or someone she admires from a distance but we don't really know since the song does not give us clear identifying details. However, this song was adapted and used in the "Sister Act" film. In that film, with the context in which it was performed for the Pope at the end of the film, we clearly see that the nuns are referring to Him as God; we derive that from the context in which the song is sung and also by who is singing the song versus the actual words themselves.

Implicit / Explicit Meanings

Implicit language has meaning that is implied and most likely is not obvious or overtly understood; rather it is a meaning that is hidden or hinted at in some artistic, poetic or symbolic manner. "Reading between the lines," is a common idiom that means gaining insight or meaning beyond the obvious words that are spoken. Someone can say one thing, yet mean something altogether different. Sexual innuendo is one example of how we use implicit language or meaning when we communicate. Poems and music are well known for having multiple meanings beyond the obvious and that is part of the beauty of the art form. Allusion, simile, and metaphor are a few of the poetic devices that you will encounter as you perform or interpret music. The person who is interpreting must often decide what to do when faced with hidden or symbolic meanings. In the Christian church, there are many phrases that are said such as the "Prince of Peace," "Lamb of God," "Lion of the tribe of Judah," and "Lily of the Valley." Many Christians know these to be synonymous names for Jesus Christ. However, suppose you are interpreting for a deaf person visiting the church for the first time that has no knowledge of the Bible or Christianity or the various names of Christ. What do you sign,-- the concept/meaning, the literal words or both?

Do you give the deaf person access to the title used and make the meaning of the title (which is not explicitly understood) clear to the deaf person? Or do you leave it as said leaving it up to them to investigate more since that is what would happen for the hearing person who is also a first time visitor and is unaware? There is no one right way to answer that question. You, as the interpreter in that situation, must decide what best serves your client in the setting and proceed accordingly. I warn you not to assume that you *have to* make it clear for the deaf person. That is a "no - no"! Do not shift into the "helper of the poor deaf person" mode of thinking. It is damaging and degrading and is not acceptable in any circumstance.

Explicit is the opposite of implicit in that explicit lyrics hide nothing. Explicit language is fully and clearly expressed or demonstrated, leaving nothing merely implied; it can also reference language that may be deemed inappropriate. Think of how some music is labeled with the explicit content warning so that parents are informed that the music contains strong language or depictions of violence, sex or substance abuse, and that parental discretion is advised. Explicit lyrics out right portray or describe any or all of the following: drug use and abuse, profanity, sexual language, violent and abusive behavior, and racist, sexist or homophobic language. Since I have not included any examples of such lyrics, if you are curious as to what explicit lyrics look like, I would suggest doing an Internet search or find a CD that has the warning label and then do a search for that musician's lyrics.

One example of explicit lyrics that I will mention later is a sample from a song by artist Eminem. I took on the challenge (speed, poetry, and rhyme) of working on the lyrics to exercise my creativity, challenge my comfort zone, and to prove to a friend that it was possible to do the song – especially since Keith Wann demonstrated "Ice Ice Baby" by Vanilla Ice as part of his ASL comedy act (which you can see on YouTube.com.) Despite its several uses of profanity, the song has a positive message and that is one of the things that drew me to the song. If *I* were going to perform this song, most likely *I* would opt for the "clean" version, which edits the profanity out.

Not all explicit lyrics are as overt as what I mentioned previously. Some are about explicit subject matter yet the specific language is not explicit; sometimes the theme is explicit but may be presented in a manner that is implicit. Artist Cyndi Lauper has recorded a song called "She Bop" which is about masturbation. Though that specific word is not used, the meaning or theme is fairly explicit even though the actual language is not explicit. ASL by nature is an explicit language. What I mean is, because it is a visual language, it is much easier to gather a meaning in many instances simply because you can "see" what is being talked about. If you are signing "She Bop", do you, knowing the song is about masturbation, choose to sign one of the several choices for male or female masturbation or do you find some "creative" way to sign it making it implicit enough to not be offensive yet explicit enough to know what is being sung about? Wow, I know. . . hard one huh? Oops! Did I just say that? Ok what I meant was I know that is a tough question to answer. (Wiping sweat from my brow.)

I personally would opt for the latter. Being more creative affords you greater latitude in your performance. You run less risk of being offensive, you increase the overall enjoyment of the songs, and you as an artist are exercising your creativity muscles, which is always a good thing; much better than going for the easy way out by simply signing "masturbate" several times, which would be funny, though possibly not effective overall.

"SHE BOP"
Cyndi Lauper

They say I better stop - or I'll go blind
Oop - she bop - she bop
She bop--he bop--a--we bop
I bop--you bop--a--they bop

Another song that has sexual innuendo and yet is not offensively explicit would be Chuck Berry's song "My Ding-a-ling." How would you reference the implied sexual body part that makes the song funny, without altering the songs meaning? After all he is not talking about the male sexual organ; he is talking about a set of silver bells on a string.

"My Ding-A-Ling-A-Ling"
Chuck Berry

Once while climbing the garden wall,
Slipped and fell had a terrible fall
I fell so hard I heard birds sing,
But I held on to My ding-a-ling

What about the songs "Proud Mary" by Ike and Tina Turner and "Puff the Magic Dragon" by Peter, Paul, and Mary? Both songs are "rumored" to be about marijuana. Would it be most effective to make that information explicit?

Note: Depending on the venue and the manner in which it is being sung/performed you may not even want to remotely imply the drug related rumor.

Scenario:
You are at a children's concert and "Puff the Magic Dragon" is performed. Do you think that is a proper venue for you to creatively imply the use of marijuana? A Saturday Night Live skit would be a more appropriate venue. When interpreting, it is important for you to keep in mind the intent of the speaker or performer. If he / she is making clear reference to the possible meaning, then you should as well. When you are the ASL performing artist, however, you have a little more flexibility, creativity and artistic license than you would as the interpreter. However, you must also be clear on your intent and your audience.

Ask:
- Who am I performing for?
- Why am I performing for them?
- Why am I doing this song?
- What do I want them to get from the song I am performing?

Once you have answers for these questions, you will be better able to decide if you should or should not make something explicit.

Unlike the Cyndi Lauper example I gave earlier, "She Bop", where the sexual references are more explicit, the marijuana reference is implicit, which is why it is rumored to be about drug use. If it were more explicit, then it would be clear and undisputed such as "**Got to Get You into My Life**", which is a song by The Beatles. According to Paul, the song was about marijuana. Another song with a drug – related reference is "**Angel**" by artist Sarah McLachlan. That song is about Jonathan Melvoin, the touring keyboard player for the Smashing Pumpkins who died in 1996 after overdosing on heroin. When listening to the lyrics, is there anything that explicitly tells you this background information? The song was written about a musician's overdose on heroin, yet the song has been used at funerals, NYC 9-11 memorials, and on TV shows. Why? Because of the melody and mood conveyed in the song?

Clearly drug overdose and 9-11 are not synonymous. So what is it about the song that makes it appeal in these certain situations despite the background story and the creative muse that inspired the song? I believe we connect to the melody and mood and the concept of death that is implied in the lyrics. What does the following piece of the lyrics mean to you? Do you see drug use being implied?

"Angel"
Sarah McLachlan

And it's hard at the end of the day
I need some distraction Oh a beautiful release
Memories seep from my veins and make me empty and weightless
and maybe I'll find some peace tonight In the arms of the angel

While we are talking implied language, I find that many times students will ask me how to sign a particular idiom much like they ask for a specific word. My response is always the same – What does it mean? Find the meaning and sign the meaning. Here are several idioms. Notice how you have the phrase that says one thing but in fact means something different. There in lies your challenges . . . do I sign what is said or what it means?

Always a bridesmaid, never a bride
If someone is always a bridesmaid but is never a bride then they never quite fulfill their ambition or goal. Even though they get close, they never manage to receive the recognition that they crave.

An old flame
An old flame is a person's "Ex," somebody that he/she has had an emotional, usually passionate, relationship with, and is still thought about with fondness and affection.

Much ado about nothing
If someone is making a lot of fuss about something trivial.

Kick the bucket / Bought the farm / Pushing up Daisies
All three of these are references that mean someone has died.

Tough cookie
Someone who will do everything that is necessary to achieve what they want.

Our regular everyday language is filled with such idioms and many of us never really stop to think about them. Well I encourage you, starting today, right now, to take more time to study and listen to what people say, and ask yourself – "What does it mean?" and "How do I sign that?"

Here are four additional examples where what is said is not what is conceptually meant:

"The Christmas Song"
Jack Frost nipping at your nose

"You Raise Me Up"
You raise me up, so I can stand on mountains;
You raise me up, to walk on stormy seas

"Colors of the Wind"
Composer Alan Menken and lyricist Stephen Schwartz - "Pocahontas" Disney soundtrack

Can you sing with all the voices of the mountain.
Can you paint with all the colors of the wind.
Can you paint with all the colors of the wind.

"Waiting on the World to Change"
John Mayer

And when you trust your television
What you get is what you got,
Cause when they own the information, oh
They can bend it all they want.

Let's look at the John Meyer song for a sec. ok? The phrase "What you get is what you got" is implying something. What is it?

Also who is the "they" that own the information and can "bend" it if they want? Bend it means to do what? I know you may be expecting me to answer the questions, but many of them I am not going to answer because that forces you to begin to use your critical thinking skills versus me giving you all the answers. Don't worry, when I teach my classes, I am always asking them (my students) questions about what something means and why. It is good training. . . get use to it. (If you really really get stuck and really want an answer, email me.)

Many religious songs have implicit language as well. The phrase "Lamb of God" is referring to Jesus but it does not say that explicitly and to a novice of Christian music and phraseology "Lamb of God" and Jesus may not be synonymous. But for the sake of our discussion -When that phrase is in a song, do you sign Lamb of God or do you sign Jesus? What about the phrase / title "Rose of Sharon", "Rock of Ages"? The list of titles and names can go on and on and remember that my way is not *THE* way... my way is merely *A* way. The audience for which I am performing / interpreting sometimes factors into how *I* perform / interpret a song. It also depends on things such as how many times the specific line is stated. Sometimes if a line like "Lamb of God" is repeated, I will sign the exact phrase the first time to give access to the phrase but then after that will sign what it conceptually means. But again, it also depends on the audience or congregation and what I am doing – interpreting or performing.

You, the performer/interpreter, must put into the song / performance what works best in that given performance and time. Remember that list of four questions to ask yourself?

- Who am I performing / interpreting for?
- Why am I performing / interpreting for them?
- Why am I doing this song?
- What do I want them to get from the song I am performing? (or from my interpretation of the song)

You must also assess what signs will best match the concepts and intent of the song and what signs would be (most clear), conceptually accurate and visually pleasing.

Now do you see why I love this musical analysis work? It really makes you think and process meanings and concepts of words and phrases. It is by improving your ability to do that, that you improve your ability to sign conceptually versus literally.

DOS AND DON'TS OF INTERPRETING MUSIC AND OR THEATER

* Do not upstage the speaker / performer(s).

* Do not dance or move excessively.

* Do obtain lyrics in advance and become familiar with and possibly work on a translation to target language i.e., transliterated or idiomatic translation.

* Do honor the Code of Ethics / Code of Professional Conduct.

* Do provide the language desired by consumers.

Do not upstage the speaker / performer(s).
You are not the actor, the speaker, presenter, nor are you the performer, so you are not to become the center of attention. Even though the deaf person looks to you for language, you are not the "star" so you must keep your ego in check and facilitate the language without upstaging.

Do not dance or move excessively.
You are not the "show"; you are not there to entertain. You should not be distracting to the audience by taking the focus from the show. Remember that no one paid admission to see you.

Do obtain lyrics and become familiar and when possible translate to target.
Regardless of your particular style, it is always good practice to get the lyrics, script, etc in advance. Do not simply go in cold without preparation. Once you obtain the lyrics or script, begin to familiarize

yourself with it. You do not necessarily have to memorize it or do a written translation, but you should become familiar enough to do a competent and effective job at interpreting it into either an idiomatic or transliterated manner.

<u>Do</u> honor code of ethics / code of professional conduct.

Become familiar with the standards and expectations of a professional interpreter and follow those guidelines according to the governing standards set by the RID and NAD.

<u>Do</u> provide target language as desired by consumers.

Your consumers may want more of an English sentence structure – transliteration – or a more ASL interpretation – idiomatic. Be aware of the difference and your skills to accommodate so the consumer gets what they desire.

How are interpreting and performing similar and dissimilar?

Now what, you may ask, does all of that have to do with our topic of performing? In many ways when you perform in ASL, the previous Do and Do Not list changes in some ways. When you are performing, -- and we will delve farther into what performing ASL means,-- you are now the star so you need not be concerned about upstaging someone else. You are now the presenter, performer, focal point so you must give as much to the performance as possible. Let's talk more about performing songs in ASL now.

PERFORMING

Performing is the act of doing something to entertain, bring enjoyment through a performance or a show. As an ASL performing artist, we therefore are using ASL to entertain our audience and possibly to educate them as well.

<u>Do's and Don'ts of performing music in ASL</u>
* Do obtain lyrics in advance.

* Do translate into target language (conceptually correct).

* Do think in terms of performing (not interpreting) so be aware of size of signs, visually pleasing choices, body language and facial expression, incorporating visual vernacular and other theatric and performance techniques that will heighten the entertainment of the show (such as dance.)

* Do not interpret the music, you are now performing it.

As a performer there are several key concepts and techniques to know and develop.

Techniques to Develop: Centering

Centering is being comfortable with who you are as a performer / interpreter and more importantly as a person. It is also being in harmony with your body, movement style and ability, sign style and ability, and overall presence. As a performer / interpreter (from now on you may not see both words "performer / interpreter" but realize that I am using them interchangeably throughout the text), you must have a sense of who you are in order to develop and to have stage presence, which enables you to entertain, educate, and inspire an audience. If you do not interest or captivate the audience, they will be bored, rather than entertained. Centering, or being centered, is pivotal to your physical presence. It is like being off balance. How much control can you have if you are off balance? How comfortable can you be if you are off balance? That moment right when you can feel yourself falling, how stable are you? Our goal is to develop the ability to be focused and centered no matter where you are performing or interpreting.

Suppose you show up for church one day and are told that your favorite musician or TV personality is speaking, -- maintaining composure and remaining calm are centering. Likewise, suppose you had rehearsed a particular set of songs with the choir and Sunday, you walk in to find that all of those songs have been replaced. Being centered means you accept the fact that you were caught off guard and that you then begin to calmly (and with focus) figure out what you can in order to do the best job you can do.

While there are many ways one can learn centering, one of the easiest is developed through the art of Mindful Breathing, and Mindfulness in general. Let me explain. . .

Having studied and taught martial arts for several years, I have found that mindful breathing is most applicable and easiest to teach to non-martial artists in order to help them become centered. Do you know the "count to ten" technique that people do in order to calm down when angry? That is a form of mindful breathing. You are focusing on the counting as you breathe and that in turn causes your anger to dissipate. Essentially, mindful breathing is a form of meditation that allows you to focus, become more aware, and calm yourself. Many of us carry far too much fear, tension, stress, worry, and confusion. Due to our hurried and chaotic life-styles, we rarely take the time to be quiet, to be still, to do the much needed introspective work and assessments that can help us live longer and better lives. Mindful breathing gives you the beginning glimpse to a world of calm, ease, and awareness, as well as, access to the reserves of power in your body, mind, and spirit. Rather than leaving an interpreting job exhausted, wore out, and suffering from neck and back pain, you can leave excited and energized feeling the kind of tired that you experience from the satisfaction in a job well done.

How to get centered
Begin by being mindful of your posture. Whether sitting or standing be aware of your posture. This is another one of those areas where we inflict undue pain and stress on our physical selves. Your spine is the part of your skeletal frame that holds you up. If it is not healthy and strong, then by default the rest of the body will be weak and ineffective. Often times when we are in resting mode, we are placing undo stress on our bodies. Poor or ineffective posture, coupled with ineffective breathing, is the cornerstones for stress, fatigue, pain and disease.

Begin the centering exercise by finding a quiet place where you can sit undisturbed for a minimum of 15 – 20 minutes. You may play some soft soothing music or ambient sounds as part of your centering; however, do not allow yourself to rely on the music. You will want to be able to center yourself at will in any location or event which means your music will not be present. Many of us are not accustomed to or comfortable with silence. Many of us, due to our dislike of silence will upon arriving home, automatically turn on the TV, radio, or music on the computer. The noise to many of us is more comforting than the silence. If that is what you habitually do, the centering in silence will be of special benefit for you.

Begin by sitting in a comfortable straight-back chair. Once you have mastered this technique, you can stand if you want or need to.

Place both feet flat on the floor. Your back should be straight but naturally straight, not a "forced military" kind of straight. Allow the natural curvature of your spine to hold you erect, keeping your head aligned atop your spine. In this seated position, rest your hands gently on your thighs, palms facing up. Eyes closed, begin to notice how you are breathing. Do not change it or force it, just notice it, become aware of it. Notice how your body moves in rhythm of the breathing cycle. Notice the rise and fall of your chest as you inhale and exhale. Notice your body's release of tension as it twitches or readjusts in the chair. It is often very difficult for us to sit still; become aware of your body and its particular challenges to remaining still. Much like the physical release of tension shown in the excess movements of your body, your mind will make adjustments as well. You will find stray thoughts entering your mind, things you need to do, people to call, appointments to keep. This is mental chatter and is natural but it is something you want to learn to control. Once you have practiced being mindful of the breath several times and you are comfortable and achieving a sense of calmness, you are ready for the next part of the training. In the next part of the exercise, you will continue to train the mind by counting your breaths. Note that if you find yourself drifting in thoughts or losing track of the numbers, do not criticize yourself. Simply return to the task, easily and effortlessly. In time you will silence the chatter.

Having observed several breaths, now consciously alter the pattern. Take a nice deep inhale, through your nose, allowing your abdomen to rise and then exhale through your mouth as your abdomen falls. Repeat this two or more times as you are comfortable.

Having now begun the more effective method of abdominal breathing, you are ready to go deeper into being centered. As you inhale, count. Your inhalation should now take a count of three to accomplish. Hold the breath for a count of one, and then exhale to a count of three. Repeat the 3-1-3 cycle several times until you are comfortable increasing the number. Once you are comfortable you will increase the length of the cycle. Remember there is no need to rush. The purpose is to center – not finish or win the race. If you keep the 3-1-3 cycle for a few days, weeks or even months, before moving on that is fine. Find your center at your own pace.

When you are ready, you will increase the inhaling to a count of five, hold the breath for three and exhale on five. Again, do the 5-3-5 cycle until you are comfortable. The next cycle is 7-5-7. Inhale to a count of seven, hold the breath for five, then exhale to seven. Never force yourself to inhale, to hold, or to exhale! Forcing the breath will keep you tense. If you find yourself unable to hold the breath, release it naturally. In time you will increase your breathing capacity. Though it is much more challenging, doing a 10-10-10 cycle of breathing is typically what I teach my martial arts students and it offers many benefits. However, even if you remain at the 3-1-3, you will still develop the ability to center and obtain benefits.

Centering allows you to release nervousness, fear, tension and stress, and increase calm, stability, confidence, focus, concentration and an overall sense of well being and peace of mind. From the centered state, you can stand or sit comfortably where you will be the best interpreter / performer of which you are capable. From this centered state you will find the foundation on which you can build increased mindfulness and physical presence.

MINDFULNESS

I would like to take a moment to comment about mindfulness as it relates to stress. Many times when we are interpreting or performing, we catch ourselves doing something we label as wrong, then we obsess over the wrong sign, missed word or phrase, other ways we could have signed or voiced the message. In those moments when we are stuck in the past, we are not being present in the Now. Mindfulness will release you from the regret of the past or worries of the future because you are only in the present. I am not saying don't think about how to better your skills by evaluating your product. What I am saying is – do not obsess over it or kick yourself for doing something "wrong." Make note, make improvements, and move on.

This can also assist you in being critical or judgmental of other interpreters or signers. We are all on various levels of skill, various levels of consciousness, and various levels of awareness. To judge or criticize someone for the manner in which they signed something speaks more to your state of being than to that person's state of being. You are choosing to be mindful of error, judgment, criticism, and ridicule. You will see people sign things in ways that you would not and you will see interpreters interpret things in ways that you would not and they will make "mistakes," as do we all at some point or another. What does it serve you or the community to focus on the negative? Choose to be mindful of improvement, support, health, healing, and being affirming.

Physical Presence

No matter where you are, as you enter a room, walk down the street, or shop in a store, your movements and mannerisms say something about who you are. Your very presence speaks volumes. Are you seen as a confident person based on your presence? Are you seen as a timid person? What about aggressive or distant? Did you know that most criminals (muggers, purse snatchers, rapists) select their victims based upon how the person carries him or herself? As a performer, from the moment you take the stage – and actually from the moment you arrive at the venue – your presence must demand or command attention. As an interpreter you must command / demand professionalism and confidence.

Interesting note is that the power of your centered presence also becomes a beneficial skill when you have it both on and off the stage. The confidence you exude will be present within you no matter if you are on or walking down a busy NYC avenue. I hope for you to have the confidence of a performer when the curtain goes up, when you have made the final bows, when the audience leaves AND even when you are shopping at Target. The confident sense of self and centered being are much-desired skills to obtain. The process along this path begins with being mindful. Become aware of your actions, your thoughts, and your emotions. What are you thinking and feeling in any given setting and why are you thinking about it? Pay attention to the thoughts you allow to enter and remain in your mind; many great teachers all agree "As you think so shall you be."

If you think defeated thoughts, you will be defeated.
If you think you can't improve your ASL, you can't.
If you think you are weak, ugly, untalented, then by your own thoughts you are what you think.

Have you ever noticed how something occurs that results in you becoming angry, then you calm down and seemingly forget about it; however each time you tell a friend the story, you get riled up almost as if you are reliving the situation all over again? Each time you tell how your boss, the guy in traffic, the waitress or the store clerk made you mad, your mind thinks about it. It, in essence, recreates the situation and your body, not knowing the difference, goes right back into "fight or flight" mode – your heart rate increases, blood leaves certain parts of the body and brain to prepare the limbs to fight or flee, digestion stops, you sweat more, your immune system is diminished. While this is a normal physiological response when we need to fight off or escape from a bear or mugger, this is not a response to which you want to daily subject your body. Repeated subjection to such stress puts your body out of harmony, out of ease and when your body is in "dis-ease"... you increase the risk of developing a disease.

"As a man thinketh so shall he be."
Proverbs 23:7

Begin to notice when you are less confident and insecure, nervous, or some how inadequate and in that moment begin to center yourself. Do the breathing exercises you just learned, and as you inhale, be more mindful and think about yourself becoming more confident. Affirm that you are feeling the way you want to feel, moving the way you want to move, signing the way you want to sign. Inhale and visualize yourself as a confident individual; and as you exhale, release the insecurity.

In addition to being mindful of your emotions, of how you think, how you behave, how you move, also become aware of how you interact on an interpersonal level with others. Are you a good listener or do you dominate conversations? Do you have a sense of humor? Do people like being around you or do they prefer to avoid you? Do you tend to think negatively or positively about life? Are you heavy footed and stomp when you walk or are you light on your feet and agile? Are you overweight or underweight, are you awkward or graceful, and are you poised and proper in your posture or do you slouch? Do you linger on the past, worry about the future, suffer in your present?

"Pain is inevitable, suffering is optional."
-Unknown

These types of self-analytical questions can assist you in learning more about yourself and the more you know about yourself, the better you can become. Also be aware of how you feel when you do things. Do feel self-conscious when you walk into a room? Why? (Get used to that "Why" question. I will be asking that a lot.) Do you feel frustrated easily over certain things? Why? What embarrasses you? Why do you feel embarrassed? What scares you? What makes you feel proud and accomplished? Those are also key questions and things to know about yourself and having the answers can be a great asset on your journey to becoming a skilled ASL performing artist, interpreter, human. Once you have mastered self-awareness, begin to observe others around you. Read their body language and read between the lines when they talk to people. The more aware you become, the more of a "master" you will also become. Not only will you be a master performer, but amazingly you will find the quality of your life enhanced as well.

"A great thought begins by seeing something differently,
with a shift of the mind's eye."
-Albert Einstein

Visually Pleasing

Part of being a master performer entails understanding the concept of being visually pleasing in your presentation. Simply put, visually pleasing is when what you are looking at is aesthetically pleasing and enjoyable to view. Have you ever looked at a room that just looked blah? Seen a color on a car that made you think who on earth would like that color? Seen a dress that you thought was ugly? Those are things that you are assessing visually as being pleasing or unpleasing. In like manner, you must assess your presence, your signs, and your performance for their visual pleasure. This applies to interpreting as well. If the speaker is eloquent, then your manner of interpreting is supposed to match, yet many of us do not think about if we are pleasing to watch, or as my grandmother would say, "Easy on the eyes."

Do you have a style that is enjoyable to watch? Do you even know what your sign style is? If not, return to practicing mindfulness. Observe your specific tendencies; you may need to videotape yourself to truly see all of your idiosyncrasies. Do you sign small, large, fast, slow, clear, or sloppy? Some people sign so conversationally that they are unclear in their interpreting style. If you are not sure about your style then do as I just mentioned and videotape yourself; asking for feedback from someone you deem skilled to give the requested feedback is also a viable option. How you sign, how you move, how you perform as a whole should be pleasing to the eye.

> "A man, who has attained mastery of an
> art, reveals it in his every action."
> -Samurai Maxim

One important thing, apart from the centering and presence we just covered, that I have found of significant impact in making your product visually pleasing is your use and awareness of ASL grammar.

The signs you choose and structure of sentence must be grammatically correct, conceptually correct, clear, and pleasing to the eye. In addition to being grammatically correct, the manner in which you sign – your presence and your style should be aesthetic, graceful, and have the ability to captivate the viewer the same way a motivational speaker or superb vocalist would do using their voice.

Ask Simon Cowell from American Idol – A singer who is not pleasing to listen to is a huge turn off to the people who are sitting there listening. Likewise, there are people who stand up to give presentations, teach classes, or deliver keynote addresses at functions whose monotone delivery is found to be boring and painful to endure. As a life long learner, I have had that experience several times. In fact, I used that model to develop my teaching and speaking style which is far from being monotone. I am what others have endearingly called – animated!

So again, I cannot stress enough the art of being mindful of self, of training, practice, study, self-evaluation. A true martial artist knows that you must train to develop the body, mind and spirit. Likewise, we as performer(s) / interpreters must train with the same diligence of a warrior if we are to excel.

"Make sure you practice the ASL language correctly...
Practice makes perfect... If you practice the language wrong,
you will execute the language Perfectly Wrong!"
-Dr. Raymont Anderson

Do whatever you need to in order to become more aware of your style, your tendencies, your strengths and any areas in need of improvement. The more you learn about yourself, the greater your skills and overall presence as an interpreter, performer, and human will be. Do not be afraid to ask someone for assistance. Sometimes, as I said, it takes asking for feedback from someone qualified to assess the areas you desire to look at.

"Knowing is not enough, you must apply;
willing is not enough, you must do."
-Maxim Osiptsov

MOVEMENT

ASL is a visual language. The signer moves not only the hands but also the fingers, arms, body, face, and head. Being consciously aware of your movement style is therefore of great benefit, as is knowing your level of comfort and discomfort with moving. Many interpreters learn to sign in the smaller signing space; signing too large is more often than not distracting and inappropriate for most interpreting settings. While this may be true for most interpreting settings, remember that it is not true for all settings or situations. For the record, many settings will require larger than normal signing space -- such as theatrical interpreting, platform interpreting at a performance (such as a musical concert). It would also be true for platform interpreting at, say, a college graduation where you are on stage before a sea of people. Your signing style will vary based upon the setting, the event, and the client. You will not sign the same at a Shakespeare festival or at a Creed concert as you would in the intimate setting of a doctor's office or departmental meeting.

While taking into account the size of your signs, you must also be aware of the speed, the fluidity, and you must also be acutely aware of clarity. Many a signed song is filled with arms swinging wildly to the music, yet the viewer has no idea what is being communicated due to the signer's style. Think of a rock singer or rapper whose words often times are unintelligible and unclear to the listeners. This is not the goal for the ASL performing artist, interpreter, or person having a conversation in ASL. At all times you want to be understood, right? If communication is being engaged, then comprehension must be a factor for the communication to be effective. I find that many times people sign unclearly because they do not have a clear grasp of the ASL parameters – hand shape, location, palm orientation, or movement, let alone facial grammar or expression. However, parameter knowledge is not to blame in all situations. It has been my experience / observation that some signers / interpreters are not clear vocally as speakers and their signs only mirror their vocal vagueness.

All communication ideally should be clear and understandable to the intended receiver of the message.

Remember that you are not signing for the sake of signing. You are signing, interpreting, or performing to either facilitate communication, to entertain, to inspire, or to motivate an audience and you do so by conveying concepts through the language of ASL. Make a conscious effort to articulate each sign like the singer or public speaker who carefully selects each word, calculates each breath, each pause, intonation, and movement of body while on stage. Are your movements adding to or taking away from the overall understanding and enjoyment? If they are, in fact, taking away from, you need to seriously consider making some changes.

DANCE

I have, over many years, seen many songs signed both as interpreted pieces and as performed pieces and I have noticed that many people have no idea what to do at certain times during a song. Maybe that is why one of the most frequently asked questions when I teach is, "What do I do when there are no words and only music?"

Musical (instrumental) preludes, interludes, and postludes, as I have experienced seem to be a major concern for many people who have no idea what to do during these musical moments; no words means no lyrics to be signed which means confusion for many people. Many people choose to do the sign for song or music during those moments. Some others will indicate what instrument they are hearing and do the sign for that instrument -- for example, guitar, drum, and piano. There are also the times when the vocalist is not singing, he/she is humming or making other sounds and people will sign "mmm" to indicate a hum, or "ooo" and "ooohhh" to indicate similar sounds. Now, for the interpreter in this situation, it is often not only acceptable but what the client expects and wants. However, I have also found that many deaf clients want more than just an "mmm" or "ooo." Keep in mind that there is a distinction between the performing and the interpreting when faced with this dilemma. Sometimes your choices as the interpreter may be more limited and that is fine. My charge to you, however, is to practice alternatives for those situations; don't always resort to the habitual easy or comfortable things to do. Step out of the box and exercise your creativity. What do you do if you do have a deaf client or congregant who wants more than the sign for music, wants more than an indication that you hear a violin, wants more than a "mmm" or "aahhhh"?

I am not here to tell you what you should or should not do when this musical situation arises. My way is not *THE* way but merely *A* way. I am offering you possible alternatives that you may not have considered previously or been exposed to. One thing that I have found to be of benefit to people is to visualize that as the performer of the song you want to imagine that you are embodying the total song for a deaf audience. You literally are becoming the song; taking the auditory experience and making it a visual one. That being the case, the audience should "see" the music on your body. One of the easiest and most effectively beautiful ways to do this is through the medium of dance.

OK ... OK... I can hear you yelling out, "But I can't dance!" Let me clarify what I mean by dance. Relax. . . take a breath. . . OK? -smile-

When most people think of dance, we think of dance styles like Ballet, Modern, Tap, or Jazz and we think of dancers or choreographers like Alvin Ailey, Mikhail Baryshnikov, Janet Jackson, Usher or Michael Jackson. Dance is traditionally thought of as some type of formal training in dance techniques. Dance is so much more than formal training. However, if in depth formal training is your desire then by all means you should pursue that; however, that depth of training may not be what you currently are seeking and it is not necessary for what we are discussing now. With that in mind, I do recommend that you spend some time studying dance elements especially if you are not planning to take a class. The reason I recommend this is because dance is as diverse as the shades of skin on the faces of humanity. If you watch videos of how various cultures dance, you will see a wide and broad spectrum of styles and it would serve you best to spend some time observing dancers in action. This study can be done in several ways. You can read books, rent instructional DVDs or DVDs of dance performances, or you can attend dance concerts -- to name a few possible ways to increase your awareness of dance.

You know, it's funny that I almost started to say that dance is movement that expresses emotion and has a sense of rhythm and flow; however, I was reminded of a video about Paul Taylor, the dancer / choreographer and founder of the Paul Taylor dance company. I recall on his video "Dancemaker," where he reminisced about doing a "dance" for fifteen minutes. In this dance piece, the interesting thing is that he stood on stage and did not move at all! The music played and he remained motionless from the time the curtain rose until fifteen minutes later when the curtain descended. That bold move on his part changed the definition of what defines or constitutes a dance piece. I tell you that only to further demonstrate the various forms "dance" can take.

Now for our purposes, since you already may not want to move, let's define dance as a form of physical musicality or rhythmically moving to the music. Dance is the music moving your body. Dance is not just about leaping, twirling, and moving in some prearranged choreographed and trained steps. Dance encompasses your entire being. Dance can be as complex as break-dancing or Ballet where the style encompasses full use of your feet, legs, hips, torso, arms, hands, and head or dance can be something as simple as walking in rhythm to the music. Dance can also be as simple and natural as swaying from side to side and I am sure you all can do something like moving your body from side to side.

I sense some continued skepticism. Remember that being comfortable in your skin, being centered, and confident are all parts of the process of interpreting, performing, and living a life in harmony. Are you comfortable in your body? Work on that level of comfort first. Once you have that level of comfort, beginning to "dance" will come much easier. There are many ways to make the transition to dancing. Your options can range from taking formal classes at dance studios, to asking people you know who have dance skills to teach you, to purchasing instructional video tapes and DVDs that you can view in the privacy of your home, reading books about dance, and something I personally find to be very helpful is watching people dance. Not simply watching, but observing with an analytical eye.

I watch music videos on BET, VH-1, and MTV. I watch PBS specials when they have dance performances like The Dance Theatre of Harlem, Bill T. Jones, and Paul Taylor. I watch movies with or about dancers such as Flashdance, Fame, You Got Served, Save the Last Dance, and movies with Fred and Ginger Rogers, Gene Kelly, and Gregory Hines. I go to see dance companies like Alvin Ailey Dance Theatre, Philadanco, Merce Cunningham, Philobolus, and Twyla Tharp. I also have DVDs of dance performances that I watch such as Desmond Richardson in "Othello."

The observations that I do are based on a technique that a martial arts instructor taught me years ago. By observing people in their daily activities, you begin to gain greater understanding of how humans move; you can also apply this to animals when you watch them as well. Much can be learned simply by observing. See if someone favors one foot or leg over the other. See where they tend to shift weight. Be aware of their posture and demeanor as someone approaches them. Notice their use of eye contact.

When the lesson was initially taught to me, it was to teach me to be observant so that I could begin to see beyond the surface. It was to help me see more than a man walking, but to see a man walking with a slight limp favoring the left leg which means the right is weak possibly due to an injury. It was to also see how people interact with one another in conversation and in physical navigating down a busy street. The lesson was also used to teach me that by observing how others move, I become more aware of how I move. Do I give off signals of being scared, a victim, or injured? As I became more proficient in observing people in everyday settings, I began to realize something my instructor tried to teach me previously about watching other martial artists in action. Simply the act of observing was affording my brain time to register the movements; my brain was beginning to be imprinted with the imagery of the techniques; new synapses were being formed, creating greater awareness of the very things I was observing. I was in essence building a library of moments that I now had access to. I was told, "As you continue to observe and practice the martial arts, the images in your mind and your actual physical techniques eventually merge becoming, in essence, one." I was becoming a better martial artist simply by watching other martial artists!

Having found that technique to be 100% accurate and effective, I began to apply it not only to my teaching of martial arts but to my creative process in the visual arts and to my skills as a public school art teacher. I began to study via observations how other artists create art. How painters move from inspiration to masterpiece. How sculptors select the clay or stone or found objects and then mold, carve, or assemble them into a work of art. I just about lived in art galleries, museums, and libraries as I looked at art of all kinds. The more I observed, I found that my skills improved. I then began to use the techniques in my art classroom. I would have my students look at paintings, sculpture, and drawings of all sorts; I would have them watch other artists draw, paint, take photographs, or sculpt. Eventually, they began to see "art" all around them as well. Their creativity and artistic vision multiplied as did their confidence.

Finding this technique of value in several areas of my life, I then applied that technique to my acting and then, as you are learning here now, to my ASL performance techniques and interpreting.

I suggest that you become a people watcher, a student of performing / interpreting; observe and study all types of performing, performers, interpreters, and signers. The more you observe, the more you fill your mind with visuals of the very thing you want to improve or develop. Do you think you can learn anything about ASL performing and interpreting from watching a magician like Criss Angel? Even though magic is not your art form, is there something you can learn from watching him? I assure you – Yes you can still learn something from watching him. There are still things to see such as stage presence, confidence and how he interacts with the audience.

For your dance abilities to increase, observe how others move. Observe the various styles from line dancing and ballet, to Afro-Caribbean and Swing. Once you become more open and aware to what the body can do, you will be able to develop an individual style based upon what your body can do and how you can incorporate that into your style of performance. Quick added note: If you observe other ASL performing artists, poets, and interpreters, your skills will also improve as I have described. By taking careful note of their style, you can begin to adapt and adopt what works for you.

ASL Visual Descriptions

As users of ASL, we are quite aware that there is a certain skill or manner involved in describing people, places, and things. We know about classifiers and how they are used; however, we (non-native signers) do not often use them out of the fear of using them incorrectly and being even more unclear. Many times, rather than use a classifier to show something, we opt for the easier method of telling, of explaining rather than describing and showing. For example, if you were going to tell your friend about a recent car accident, you have the option of relaying what happened by saying, "I saw a horrible accident yesterday on the way to work. This red Pontiac GTO cut in front of this blue BMW. The Pontiac hit the front end of the BMW sending it spinning across the street where it slammed into a tree and the Pontiac, barely damaged, just drove away." Or you could say, "Yesterday there was a car accident and one of the cars left the scene." Both versions tell me the basis of what occurred; one, however, is more descriptive than the other. The first version, having more details, gives me a clearer picture of the accident versus the second, which I could have envisioned as a ten-car pile up on the interstate. When you relay a story, are you more direct and tell the story or are you more sensory and describe the story? Do you tell me that the cruise was pleasant and you enjoyed yourself or do you give me a sense of the sounds, the scents, and the sights?

If we wanted to completely describe the above car scene in ASL we would make full use of classifiers and "show" what happened. We would incorporate the appropriate handshapes for a vehicle; once we establish which car is which, we would "show" what happened to each car, the tree, and possibly even include some bystanders or other cars on the street – instead of the bland method of telling and explaining. Think about professional storytellers who read to children. The more interesting ones are those that become fully immersed in the story and take you, the listener, on the journey with them. They use vivid, colorful, and expressive language that allows you to "see" and "feel" the experience.

When I am teaching or working with my performance company one phrase or "Rayism" they often hear is "Show me, don't tell me." Seeing it happen is by far much more interesting than just being told. ASL is very much like cinematography, which will be discussed (in the section on) Visual Vernacular. In the mean time, take full advantage of all that American Sign Language has to offer, and you will become a more skilled user of the language. "How do I develop this skill?" By now you can almost predict what I am going to say, can't you? ☺smile☺ Rather than tell you what I have already told you, I will give you a few new exercises that I believe will be of assistance. If you want to develop your "describing" skills, begin with these three exercises: Photo descriptions / Floor plans / Storytelling.

Photos descriptions

Begin to see, think, and speak as a more visual person. When you give directions, tell the person what he/she will see. One way that I found to help develop the "visual muscles" is to work with magazines, catalogues, brochures, books, or anything that has wonderful photos in them. The advertisers, more than likely, did not have ASL exercises in mind when they created them, but they are excellent tools that assist our eyes and mind in becoming more visual. Take a picture, such as several of my drawings (which I have included for you to use in order to practice), and train yourself in thinking how you would describe them to someone. You can go beyond thinking about *how*; you can actually practice describing them. One good way to begin your practice is to describe the picture in writing or verbally (in your native language) first. Both the written and verbal descriptions are flat and two-dimensional, but for many of us, that is what we are most accustomed to. In order to describe it in ASL – in three-dimension – be aware that as you view the picture, you will have to think in terms of size, colors, shapes, directions, and points of view.

Look at the several samples I have provided. Begin to train yourself to not only see it in your mind clearly but to see it so clearly in your mind that you can then describe what it is that you see. You should see it in such a clear manner that when you recreate it, someone not seeing the image will be able to see it clearly based upon your demonstration. The first few examples are of several drawings that I have done of comic book characters. I have included them because of their exaggerated poses, action, clothing, and style. The images are a visual exercise to challenge you and develop your skills. I hope you enjoy. ☺

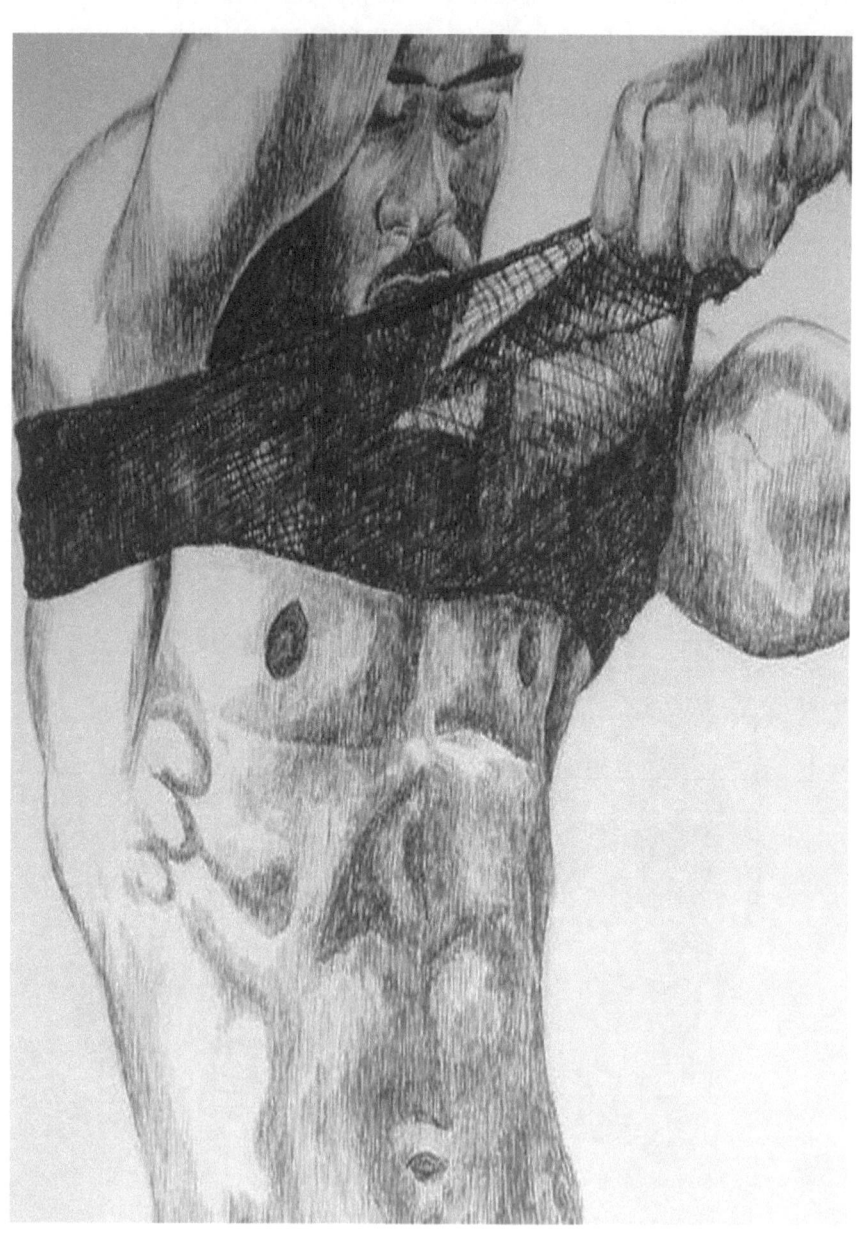

Now, having experimented with several of my provided examples, let's take it one step further. Suppose you have one particular image, but it looks similar to another in some way. How do you make a distinction for the observer? Here is a more practical example: Suppose you are telling someone that you want a pair of shoes, but there are several similar styles. How do you make sure they know which shoes you want? How do you make sure your shoe selection is clear? There are four women in the front of the auditorium with red hats and black blouses. How do you clarify the one to which you are referring? Okay, back to the drawings. If you are describing one of the drawings, you must be very clear how you set the scene, correct? For example, there were three drawings of Spiderman. Simply saying that it is a picture of Spiderman swinging on a web would not suffice. Your description must include several other key factors so that the receiver of your message knows precisely to which drawing you are referring. Otherwise, you are potentially going to confuse the viewer. Another question I am often asked with respect to directions and descriptions is, "How do I set it up? Do I set it like I see it or opposite?"

I learned that you should always describe from your point of view. If you are giving directions, they are from your POV (Point of View.) East is to your right — not their right — and west to your left, not theirs. See it, and describe it as you see it, from your POV. Descriptions also are told from the general and large to the small and detailed. For example, do not start with the pattern on clothing before you have established what you are talking about. Let's look at a few more examples.

Next are two examples of the same drawing. I altered one just to make your observation and description skills more keen as you practice how to set the scene in a manner that would allow me, the observer, to know which one you are describing.

So, did you find it easy to describe either picture? Did you find the changes in location of the bamboo, the sword, the fallen adversary, the missing child in the second drawing difficult to set up? Did you even notice the child missing in the second one? Many people don't even realize he is not in the second drawing and you cannot describe something that you, yourself, are not aware of. It is like the FedEx logo. Have you ever noticed the arrow in the logo? Many people are unaware it exists. Look at the negative space (the white area) between the E and the X the next time you get a chance and see if you notice it. Ask your friends. You might be surprised by the number of people who never notice it.

Let's try something not quite as simple as the previous drawings. Find a partner to work with. Then, observe the four similar images I have provided. Once you have them clearly in your mind, you are going to select and describe only ONE so that the person you are describing it to can select the correct one.

I find that many people are stuck when it comes to describing such images in ASL. If that is also where you feel challenged at present, stop for a moment and practice how you would describe them in writing, then practice doing so verbally. This, I find to be very helpful for those hearing people who have a challenge with verbal descriptions as well. I notice that such challenges occur often with hearing people who are less visual. So practice now, describe one of these so that someone knows exactly which one you are talking about. All of them are peace symbols and all of them have flags on them, in some fashion, and all of them have red, white, and blue colors (which I changed to gray tones). So how do you differentiate one from another?

Before you begin to describe, do not take for granted that the person knows of, or is familiar with, the peace sign in the first place. You may say "peace sign" and people could possibly envision several other symbols for peace based upon their backgrounds and personal experiences. Again, take a look at them. See them for the "first time." Begin to see the line thickness, locations of colors (shades of gray), direction of lines and shapes. Once you can see it clearly in your mind, you can begin to describe it.

Now having practiced, it is time to transfer that written / verbal skill of describing to the visual. Begin thinking about and practicing with hands up (meaning to sign it), how you would describe these in ASL. What hand shapes would you use? What classifiers? What, if anything, needs to be explained before you can go into the details of the symbol? What if you did not or could not even say peace symbol – would that limit your description? It shouldn't. Many times you may be in a situation where someone else does not (or you do not) know a "word" and you will have to describe it. Take the peace sign for example. Someone has no idea what it is. So you describe it to them. Someone does not know the word unicorn, or fairy or surfboard, so you describe it to him or her. In each of these, and more, you would have to describe versus tell.

Here are a few more exercises in describing images. The first exercise is to demonstrate what I meant when I said that you start large and work your way to the small. For the sake of demonstration, let me show you the opposite and how truly confusing it can be to start small first.

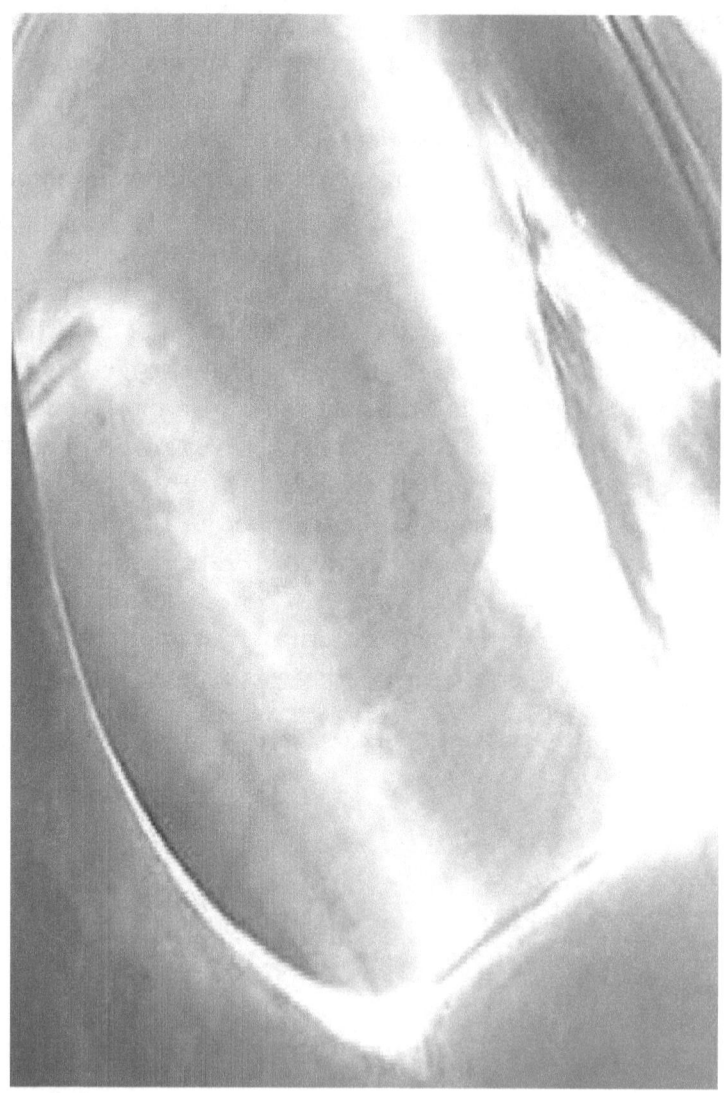

What is this photo of?

What are you able to tell from what you see?

What do you not know?

Okay, try the second one after zooming farther out.

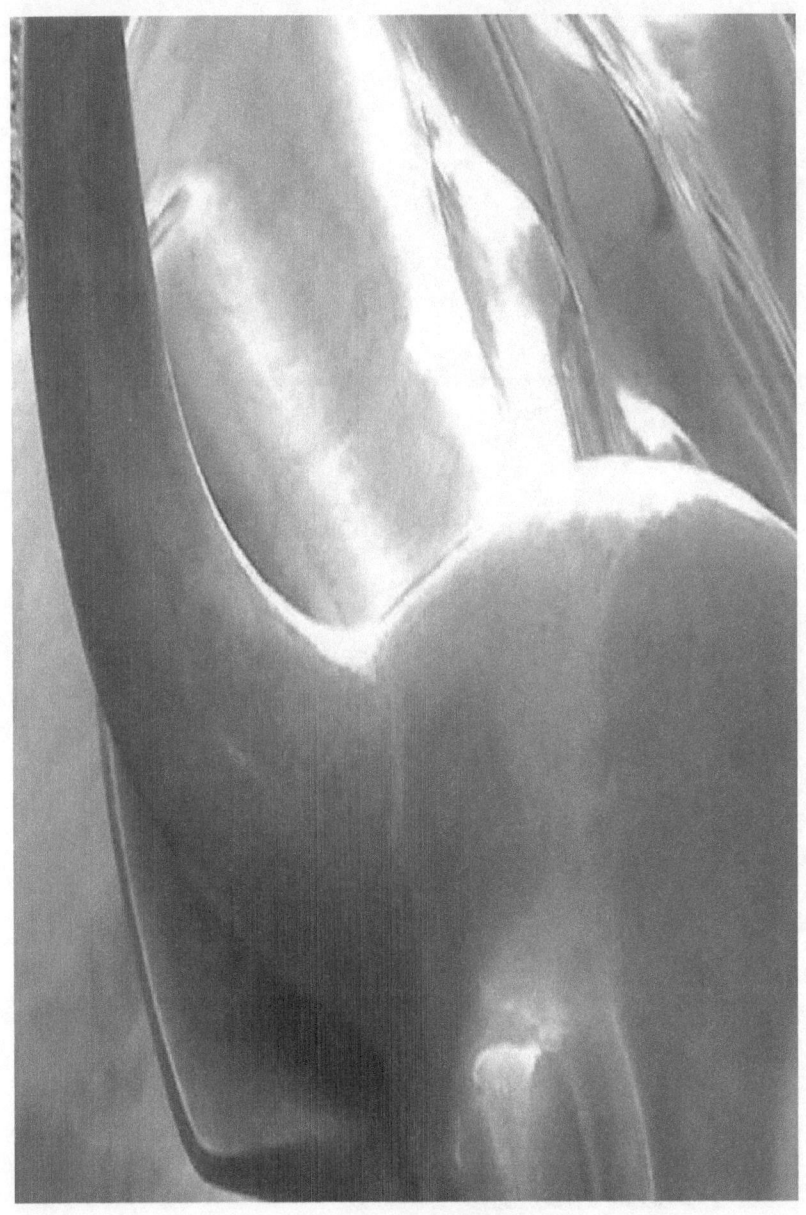

Any better?

What is it now?

How much can you really decipher and describe?

You have much more information to work with now, right?

Now you can actually begin to tell what the image is.

Here is the final zoomed out photo I took of the Bowling Green Bull in NYC.

I hope you can now see clearly that going from small to large can be confusing and unproductive. Clearly, it is most effective to start large and work your way to smaller details.

This second exercise uses another series of photos I took while on a trip to NYC and Pennsylvania. This time, I am using similar images for you to work on distinguishing point of view and being aware of how things can change depending on your point of view. Then, work on distinguishing the various details of images that are similar, much like the drawings of Spiderman that I used earlier and the Peace Symbols you just worked with.

How do you differentiate between two images of the same object when the details are given from different points of view? Have you ever known several people who witnessed an accident or event, yet each of them had different renditions of the SAME event because of their individual points of view?

Okay, on to the images. Be aware that they are similar to each other; therefore, you have to be more mindful of how to set them up.

Point of view 1:

What is the picture of?

What are you able to tell about the picture from
the second view that the first did not reveal?

What do you see from one angle versus another
and how do you set that up visually?

Point of view changes the image.

Point of view 2:

What do you see from various angles?
Point of view nearly always changes the image.

This next series of exercises are different, yet similar. You will see what I mean once you see the images. I have a real life experience that inspired me to include them, in case you are asking, "Why would he...?" I'll answer in a second. For now, look at the images, and as we have discussed, see them and visualize them, then describe them.

Similar:

Set A

See the images, the shapes, the placements of stones, the textures, angles, and groupings and begin to work on how you would describe them.

How do you distinguish one tree from another or one grave marker from another?

My father (Charles H. Anderson) transitioned on October 14, 2002 and I had not visited the cemetery for over a year after the funeral. I decided one day, as part of my grieving process, to go to the site. I went, and as I looked around, I could not find the grave marker. I called my brother Tye who described the location to me. Little did I realize that that brief interaction would inspire an entire exercise, or lesson, in visual descriptions. I eventually found his grave despite having no marker. During a later visit, I looked out over the cemetery and noticed the many similarities and differences in the scenery. As I looked around, I began to conceptualize from a cinematographic perspective how detailed a director is in his/her vision of a film and how we, as interpreters, ASL storytellers, and performing artists must be descriptive as well.

Let's look at another observation I made while I was an art student in the late '80s and an aspiring filmmaker / actor (which I still am.)

Similar:
Set B

A door is a door is a door?
Suppose you are on a TV game show and you have to tell your teammate
which door to enter and all they have is your description of the door.

Floor plans

Giving directions from point A to point B is also an excellent way to enhance your description skills, especially since ASL students tend to find directions "oh so challenging." Here I have included two generic floor plans for you. Your challenge, once again, is to describe them. You can do so in writing first. Then verbally describe the layout of the house before doing so in ASL, or you can jump right to the ASL. Be mindful of right and left, items that are parallel to one another, which way a door opens in or out, and your particular point of view as you travel through the house.

Once you have practiced using these plans, think about your own apartment, house, office space, or bedroom. How do you describe the layout of the space? Where are things located? How do you describe the décor and placement of furniture? As with the previous exercises, consider what handshapes and classifiers you can use in your descriptions. What, if anything, do you need to add to make the description clear and concise? Suppose you are in church and a friend introduces you as a landlord to a friend of his. She is looking for a new apartment and asks you about your rental property. How do you go about describing your rental property in ASL to the potential deaf tenant so she can "see" the space without actually entering it?

Once you have done the floor plans, another thing you may want to experiment with — that I have not included here — is describing clothing or furniture. Get a catalogue from any department or furniture store such as IKEA or JCPenny and practice describing one living room set versus another one, this desk versus that one, this entertainment center, blouse, shoe, suit, or wedding gown versus that one.

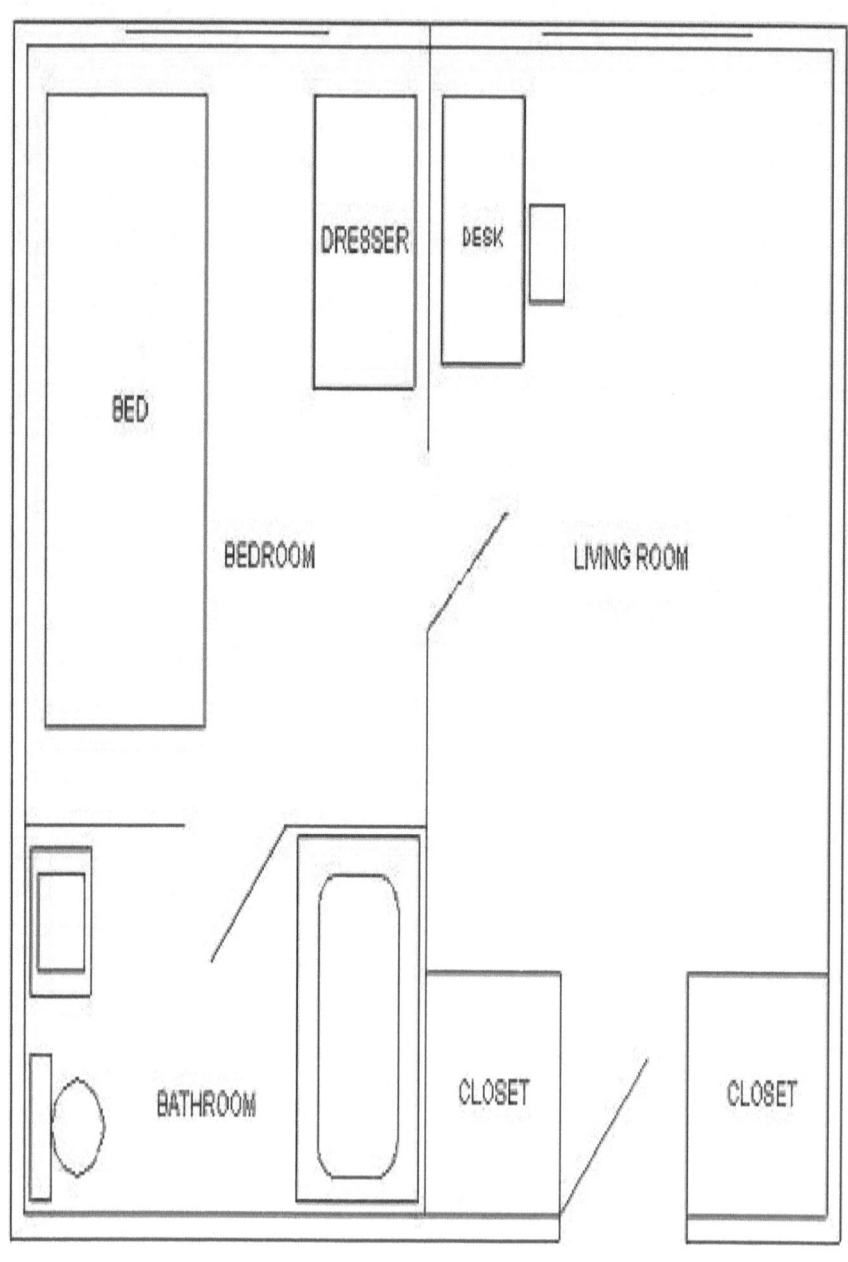

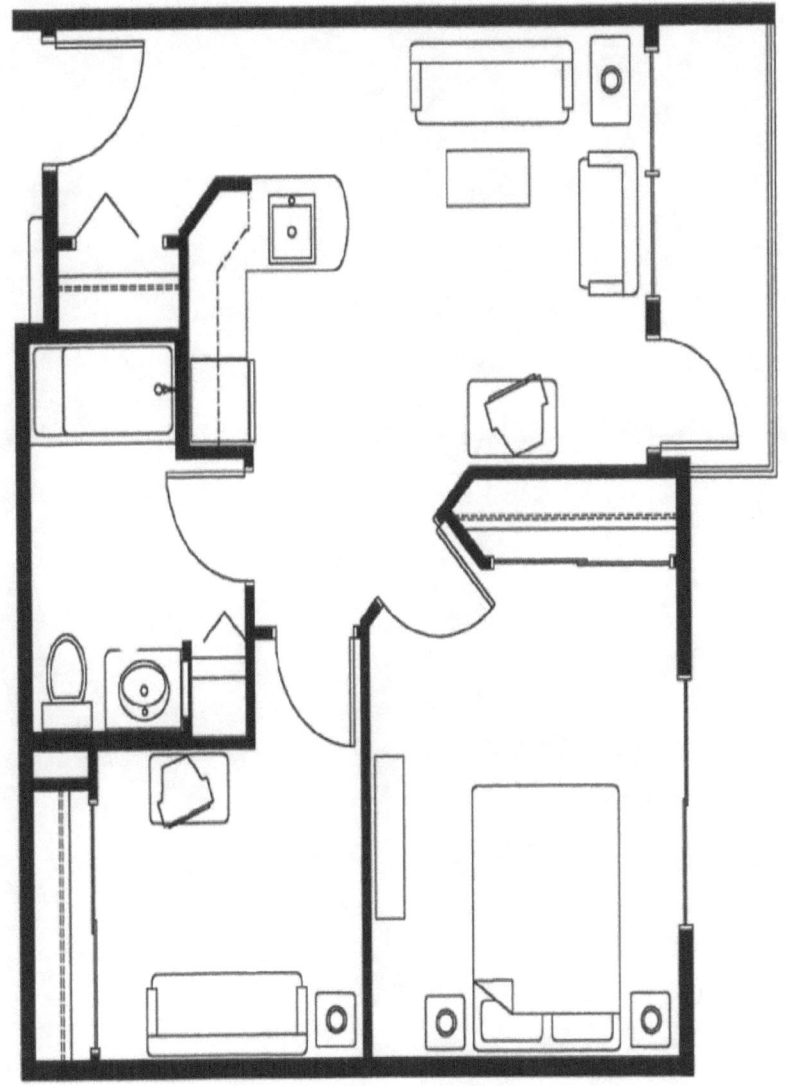

As you have figured out by now, I am sure, the first layout was much easier to describe than the second. What made the second more difficult? It is more difficult because there is more detail to that layout. There are more doors, more walls, and more furniture, all of which make for more thought-out and planned descriptions. I cannot stress the value of learning to set a scene. Many times, as interpreters, and as ASL performing artists, a location is described, and a scene is set; and in order for it to be understood, you must establish the locations clearly.

Storytelling

Telling a story is more than simply relaying an event that has occurred; you are not a news reporter when you are telling a story. An effective storyteller weaves images into the mind of the audience solely by the words used and the manner in which those words are spoken. For our purposes here, I want you to be mindful of how *you* tell stories. Are you the type of person people ask to tell stories? When you and a group of your friends do something—say go on vacation—are you the one that people want—and ask—to tell the stories of your travels? Are your stories flat and uninteresting or are they colorful and active? No matter your current level of skill, you can develop your "verbal" storytelling skills by working on a few key ingredients.

- Vocal style – Do you speak in a monotonous fashion or does your voice have range, interest, and change based on character and emotion?
- Body / movement style – Do you tend to stand still or are you more animated when telling a story? Do you include gestures?
- Language style – Do you use words that elicit sensory imagery? Do you use adjectives that give not only a visual sense of the scene but a feel for it as well? Do you tend to tell the story or do you show it through language use? Example: "He walked in the dark room and sat down," versus "Nervously, he crept into the dimly lit room. From what he could see, as his eyes began to adjust to the darkness, it appeared to be a den of some sort—possibly the resident's home office. The air was hot and stale—as if death had found a new home. His instincts said not to remain in this room but his body—tired and heavy like stone—needed to sit, just for a moment, to rest."

Have someone videotape you telling the story of *Goldilocks and the Three Bears* or *The Three Little Pigs*. If you cannot videotape, then record yourself telling the story into a tape recorder; though it will not capture your body movements (or lack of), it will give you a good sense of what you are doing vocally. Afterwards, watch the tape or listen to it. What do you notice? Were there definite moments when you took on the role of narrator? Goldilocks? Each of the three bears? Did you hear any difference at all? Each character has a distinct role in the story. Each character has a distinct appearance, different voice, and behavior. In your story, do you give the audience access to these aspects of the story? Did you set the stage, so to speak (i.e., did you give the audience a visual of the setting for the story?)

You can do this with any story, whether it is *Goldilocks and the Three Bears*, *Little Red Riding Hood*, "Gluscabi and the Wind Eagle," "The Matrix," "Jesus and the Woman at the Well", or your last vacation. A story is a story is a story and they all have similar elements.

- Setting – where the story occurs.
- Characters – people (or animals) in the story.
- Characterization – the way an author creates and brings the people in their story to life. For many authors, playwrights, directors, and storytellers, their characterizations of the characters may be what is called "flat" or one-dimensional, (i.e. the good guy is always the hero and the bad guy is always the villain); or they may be "round" or complex characters (i.e., they have many sides to them: compassionate, miserly, mean, rude, beneficent, etc. They may also be "static" (meaning they don't change at all during the story) or "dynamic," in that they change, grow, evolve during the story.
- Plot – the events that occur in the story; also referred to as the storyline.
- Theme – the message that is in the story or what the story is about; the central concept or the controlling idea. While not all stories have a central concept, theme or moral, I do believe that all stories have a message.
- Point of view – the perspective or angle that the story is being told / from whose slant the story is told.

The three main types are:

First person: The story is told by someone who identifies himself as "I" and is usually a character in the story. This point of view allows you to know the mind of one specific character but not the others.

Third person: The story is told by someone who is not a character in the story and identifies the characters as "he", "she", or "them." You don't find out anything more than the obvious things that can be seen, heard, or known by any casual observer.

Omniscient view: A third person device used is where the story is told by someone who is not a character in the story, but can know everything about every character in the story. Omniscient knows what they think and feel, as well as, what they see and hear.

Not every story follows the same distinct plot structure; the basic sequences of events in a story are:

1) Exposition: the beginning of the story- where the storyteller "sets the stage." It is in this part of the story that the situation of the characters is introduced and explained; the who, what, when and where is introduced; it further leads up to the development of the plot.

2) Rising Action: the series of actions and / or complications that result in the conflict or obstacle for the main character of the story. It is in this part of the story where we see drama as the tension builds, and the story progresses towards the climax.

3) Climax: usually the most exciting point in the story because it is the turning point where the conflict comes to a head; the high point in the story where one side usually dominates the other.

4) Falling Action: if the rising action can be seen as a roller coaster climbing the track to the top, then the climax can be seen as reaching the top. And so it is that the falling action is the descent on the other side—the events that happen after the climax that usually wrap up the story and lead to the conclusion.

5) Resolution: also called the conclusion or denouement; the point of closure. It is when the conflict is worked out; it is the *end of the story*.

In written works, authors will often use flashbacks or foreshadowing to build suspense. You can start in the middle of a story and use flashbacks, which are narration of events that have occurred earlier in the story. Using them can sometimes make a story more interesting and build more suspense. The other technique that is used is foreshadowing, which provides hints in a story about what happens later; this is also used to build suspense. Both techniques can also be employed in verbal / oral storytelling and ASL storytelling.

Having this basic understanding of storytelling will now give you a solid foundation upon which to improve your own storytelling techniques. Here are two story samples. Which would you say is better or more effective?

STORY A:

Back in the late 70's early 80's, I use to watch PBS pretty often. Two of my favorite late night PBS regulars were British comedians - Benny Hill and Dave Allen. As a young teen, I found British humor moderately titillating and extremely funny. I was allowed to stay up until 11:30 PM during the week; Benny Hill was on from 10:30 – 11 and Dave Allen from 11 – 11:30. So, every night I would sit in the kitchen and watch them while drinking tea and eating cookies, usually ginger snaps. To this day, I still dip my cookies in hot tea.

Well, one night as I stood to turn the TV off, I noticed someone sitting in the living room. There was an armchair right beside the door and, from where I was standing, I could see a section of the chair. I could also see someone, a woman—sitting in the chair. Mind you, there was only one woman living in our house at that time and I know the person I saw was NOT my mother.

I continued to walk to the TV and, after turning it off, I looked back down the hall and noticed the woman was now gone. I dismissed it since I was tired and ready for bed.

About a week later, one of my brothers was in the kitchen sitting in my usual spot. I noticed that he had a machete leaning against the wall and I was curious to know why. So, pointing at the machete, I asked, "Tye, what's up?"

"Over the last two weeks, I keep getting the feeling that someone else is in the house and I have seen someone in the living room."

I began to feel goose bumps and as the hair on my neck raised, he continued. "And I decided that if it ever comes for me, I have protection and if I swing and it don't fall, I can still use it to smash the window out and I can run!"

I could tell from his expression that he was as serious as a heart attack!

I began to wonder if I wanted to even bother watching my shows that night. When Tye left me alone in the kitchen, and took his machete with him, I opted to turn in early.

After a week or so of no laughs, I dismissed the thought of ghosts and night visitors and returned to my evening routine. I needed my fix of British comedy. 11:30 came quicker than usual—or so it felt. I put my teacup in the sink and threw away the napkin. After putting the cookie bag in the cupboard and turning the TV off, I saw her again! I don't remember if I even turned the kitchen lights off; I know I raced past the living room and dove in my bed and under the covers without looking back.

The next morning I spoke to my parents about the apparition that both Tye and I seemed to be plagued by. As my mother was making breakfast, I approached her first—appealing to her motherly concern for the child's well-being.

"Mom, can we move?"

She did not respond. So I repeated my question: "Mom, can we move?"

"Boy hush."

"No for real, I want to move. I think our house is haunted. Can we move please?"

"You can move. Move your butt to the table and get ready to eat breakfast!"

Hearing the shift in her voice and the colorful adjectives she added (which I have omitted from my retelling of my story) I decided it was best to go sit down as I was instructed.

I turned my attention to my dad. He had just finished reading the newspaper and was about to begin the crossword; I whispered so my mother would not hear me.

"Dad, can we move?"

"What, what did you say?"

Increasing my volume a bit, "I said can we move?"

As my dad replied, my mother turned and gave me "The Look."

"Did you ask your mother?"

"Yeah and she told me to move my butt to the table."

He laughed.

"Why do you want to move? You don't like this house?"

"I think it's haunted."

"What?"

I proceeded to explain the events that had transpired over the last three months. He sat patiently and listened before he spoke. My dad always did that before he gave his words of wisdom.

"Well, I don't think moving is the best choice under the circumstances. This woman you and Tye seem to be seeing has not done anything to either of you and she has had ample time and opportunity, so it would seem that she is not a malevolent spirit, and therefore nothing to run from. In fact, you should invite her into the kitchen for some tea and cookies one night." He then paused, smiled a bit and continued, "While you are at it, ask her for the lotto number for next week so we can hit the big million jackpot, ok?"

As my parents then laughed, I sulked and ate my bacon and eggs.

About a week later, there I was again—laughing uncontrollably, first at Benny Hill and then at Dave Allen. At 11:30, my laughter ceased. I did my clean up and turned the TV off and was about to dart upstairs again, when I heard my father's voice telling me to talk to the apparition. My parents were big on the "face your fears philosophy," so I stood my ground and, in the strongest trembling voice I could muster, I called to her.

"Hello, Miss. . . yooo hooo. In the living room, do you want some tea and cookies before I go to bed?"

I closed my eyes, fearing a gust of wind was soon to envelope me as a longhaired wicked female spirit floated into the kitchen. To my relief, there was no wind and no evil sprit; however, I still felt the need to confront this fear.

I walked down the hall and into the living room. I stood in the middle of the room and looked at the chair, which was empty of course. I looked around the room. The entire room was still and quiet. As I turned to see my reflection in the huge wall mirror opposite the door and the chair, I noticed that someone was sitting in the chair and she was beginning to stand up.

Now I could tell you that I was scared, but scared and terrified don't seem to come close to what I felt as I stood motionless, watching her, in the mirror's reflection, stand and begin to approach me. Looking at her in the mirror, she was now standing about six feet from me. Somehow, I found the courage to turn around. Thankfully, she was not there. I am sure I would have peed in my pants if she had been.

The old saying "curiosity killed the cat," never really applied to me until now, because I SHOULD have left the room and gone to bed; instead, I turned back to look in the mirror again, and sure enough, clear as day, she was standing there. This time, she was even closer and began to raise her hand to touch my shoulder. Again I turned, praying that she would not be there, but she was there! She was not a reflection this time. She was a five-foot, pale-skinned, translucent woman, wearing a long wedding-like gown; and she had deep blue eyes and bright red lips, and she was about to touch my shoulder!

Now, please don't go telling anyone this—because it is embarrassing enough to tell you—but I did, in fact, pee all over myself and half the floor, probably, as I ran through her and out of the house. I cowered in a corner on the front porch until I felt my mother's swift hand slapping me upside the head the next morning, telling me to get in the house and to get washed up!

No one has seen the woman since, but to this day, foot steps can be heard pacing in the attic, which—as I found out from doing some research at the library—was where the daughter of the previous owner committed suicide on her wedding day when her fiancée left town with a maid of honor.

STORY B:

When I was young, I always played with a small toy electric organ. I loved making music. One day, I was playing with it. My mother went to the store. I stopped playing and took a nap. When she came home, she called my name and woke me up. I knew she'd bought chocolate milk, which was one of my favorite drinks. I jumped out of the bed and ran down the stairs. I tripped and fell. The organ was sitting on the floor where I had left it. I hit my head on the corner of the organ and busted my head open. Blood went everywhere. My mother and brother rushed me to the hospital. A prejudice nurse told us to wait. My mom punched her and knocked her out. The doctor gave me stitches and a sucker for being calm and not crying. The security officers were talking to my mother to calm her down and the nurse had ice on her black eye.

Which story has more effective storytelling elements?
Which story sets the scene more vividly?
Which story has more character development?

I hope you selected story A.

In order to be an effective storyteller you have to have material to work with. You have to be clear in your descriptions of location, characters, and events.

Now let's go to your next step, which is making the verbal or written story visual using ASL.

ASL Storytelling

ASL Storytelling is as much an art as verbal/oral storytelling; it is not simply the telling of an event as you would in casual conversation. Storytelling involves so much more than just talking conversationally; and in terms of ASL storytelling, it involves much more than just signing. Telling a story in ASL involves many of the same elements as verbal storytelling, and the use of these various techniques to make the story effective, interesting, and entertaining. In ASL, the person "shows" you the story versus "telling" you the story. They employ that cinematographic skill I mentioned earlier and will revisit again later. I have no idea if you have ever seen an ASL storyteller, but whether you have or have not seen an ASL storyteller, it is now in your best interest to make every effort to research, watch and observe ASL storytellers with this new information in mind. Quintessential Deaf ASL storytellers like Manny Hernandez (better known as Manny ASL), Trix Bruce, Nathie Marbury, Bernard Bragg and Gil Eastman, are par excellence and a must see. There are also hearing ASL storytellers like Lou Fant, whom I mentioned previously for his performance of "Jabberwocky." There is also Austin Andrews, also known as AWTI, whose youtube. com videos "Deaf Ninja 1 – origin" and "Deaf Ninja 2 - DN versus TF" are beyond extraordinary.

Let's go over some things storytellers do so we can see some of the things that can assist us as we increase our awareness of storytelling in ASL. Then we can begin to incorporate into our use. In going through the story you want to tell—and for it to be clear, interesting, and effective—you should identify several things. Let's look at the following story, which most of us already know, as a practical example: "Goldilocks and the Three Bears." This will be our working example, then we will look at story A from the previous section.

Who are all of the characters (both the minor and the major ones?)
-Goldilocks, Papa Bear, Mama Bear, Baby Bear

What is the story about?
-A young girl's intrusion into the bears' home and their discovery of her intrusion.

Where does the story occur? Where does everything take place?
-In the home of the Three Bears, which is located in the woods.

More specifically, where in the home do the events occur?
-Kitchen, Living room, and Bedroom.

When does the story happen and does the time change? Does everything occur in one day or over a few days? Does it happen all in the morning or over a few hours during the day?

-Depending on who is telling the story, it happens from early to late morning. Mama Bear was making breakfast and the Bears went for a walk to let the food cool. In your telling of the story, lunch or dinner could be used in place of breakfast.

Who is doing what and what happens?
-Mama Bear makes porridge. The Bears leave the house to walk while porridge cools. Goldilocks comes to the house, finds the food, and tastes all, but eats only one completely. She then goes to the chairs, sits on all, and breaks one. She goes to the beds, lays on all, and falls asleep on one. The Bears return home, notice the food, the chairs, and the beds and find her. Then, depending on the version of the story, they do something to her or she escapes.

Once you have this general information, you can begin to construct the story by building upon the skeletal structure. Formulate your sentences by setting up how you want to tell the story.

For example, your intro could sound like:

"A long time ago, deep in the magic forest, there was a small, quaint wood cabin where a family of three bears lived – Papa Bear, Mama Bear, and Baby Bear."

Once you have the entire story fleshed out, you can begin to structure it visually according to ASL grammar and an idiomatic translation. Remember to "show me, don't tell me." Show me the forest and the house by using appropriate classifiers; show me where the house is in relation to the surrounding trees; show me Mama making porridge; show her distinct mannerisms; show me how she decides to take the family for a walk to let the food cool. Show me the characters and how they behave, how they move, and how they sign, as you become the characters and role shift to show a dialogue. Incorporate classifiers to show the size and appearance of the house, the trees, bowls, the style of chairs and beds. It is very boring to simply say, "Goldilocks sat on Papa Bear's chair but she did not like it because it was too hard." It is more interesting to say, "Goldilocks, having eaten all the porridge from Baby Bear's bowl, decided to sit down and rest. She walked into the living room and saw three very unique chairs. One was very big and made of hard oak. The second was a regular, medium-sized chair, looked very fancy and was covered in soft velvet cushions. The third chair was the smallest, with a thin pillow on the seat. Goldilocks decided to try the big one first. She did not stay seated very long, because the hard wooden seat was very uncomfortable for her."

That second one is more elaborate and more interesting, yet it is still a narrator telling you what happened. Your task as an ASL storyteller is to SHOW all of that. How do you show the chair, the cushion, her discomfort, the moving from one chair to the next, the breaking of the small chair? How do you SHOW it? You show it by role shifting from narrator to character at key moments and via gestures and acting like the characters. Remember, ASL is a "show me," visual language and is three-dimensional, versus the linear "tell me" language we read or hear.

Let's do an exercise. Let's start with little info, then build and work on developing those "show me" skills.

He walked home.

The man walked home.

The tall man walked home.

The tall man with the long dark trench coat walked home.

The tall man with the long dark trench coat staggered slowly as he struggled to get home.

Struggling through the dark city streets, the tall man staggered; his steps labored and off balance, his long trench coat—blowing half off his shoulders—flapped in the wind.

See how you can move from the boring and flat to the more vivid? And with the vivid, you have so much more to work with as you set the scene and the character.

How can you show this?
What classifiers might you use to show him staggering?
How would you physically become / act like the man struggling to walk and keep your balance?
How would you show the dark city streets?

These types of questions apply to every story and every song you do.

Let's go back now and look at story A again and begin to ask those important questions so we can build it visually.

Who are the characters?
When does the story take place?
Where does the story take place?
What happens to the characters?

As you are answering these questions, begin to think about how you would set up the locations, show the actions and show the emotions and dialogues.

STORY A: [with example of one possible gloss]

Back in the late 70's early 80's, I use to watch PBS pretty often.
HAPPEN LONG AGO 1978, 79, 1980, 82 ABOUT, I TEENAGER, WATCH TV YOU – KNOW PBS? I WATCH OFTEN.

Two of my favorite late night PBS regulars were British comedians – Benny Hill and Dave Allen.
THAT PBS, HAVE 2 PROGRAM I LOVE, FAVORITE WATCH WHAT? MAN NAME, B-E-N-N-Y-H-I-L-L OTHER MAN NAME D-A-V-E-A-L-L-E-N, TWO-THEM FUNNY MEN WHERE? COUNTRY ENGLAND.

As a young teen, I found British humor moderately titillating and extremely funny.
REMEMBER ME YOUNG, TEEN. TWO-THEM, THEIR PROGRAM VERY-FUNNY ALSO I LIKE WHY? THEY HAVE JOKE ABOUT SEX THINGS, I ENJOY.

I was allowed to stay up until 11:30 PM during the week; Benny Hill was on from 10:30 – 11 and Dave Allen from 11 – 11:30.
B-E-N-N-Y-H-I-L-L START TIME 10:30, 11 FINISH. D-A-V-E-A-L-L-E-N START TIME 11, 11:30, FINISH. PERFECT WHY? DURING WEEK, MY BEDTIME 11:30.

So every night I would sit up in the kitchen and watch them while drinking tea and eating cookies, usually ginger snaps.
HAPPEN EVERY NIGHT, KITCHEN I SIT, T-V I WATCH. ALSO HAVE TEA CL:C-left hand, AND COOKIES CL:B-small pile of, I gesture taking cookie dipping in tea and eating them.

To this day I still dip my cookies in hot tea.

THAT gesture taking cookie dipping in tea and eating them, I SINCE. NOW STILL? SAME-OLD nod head.

Well, one night as I stood to turn the TV off I noticed someone sitting in the living room.
HAPPEN ONE NIGHT, I WATCH-TV FINISH, I STAND-UP. CL:1 walking towards TV. I CL:FF eyes looking, NOTICE WHAT? PERSON THERE, LIVING ROOM, SIT.

There was an arm chair right beside the door and from where I was standing I could see a section of the chair and could see someone, a woman, sitting in the chair.
THAT ROOM, DOOR CL:BB doorway, THERE immediately to the left, HAVE CHAIR. I SEE PERSON ALL BODY? NO. KNOW CHAIR, CL:CC describing the arms of the chair, I SEE PERSON, THEIR ARM. OH-I-SEE, index WOMAN index, nodding.

Mind you, there was only one woman living in our house at that time and I know that the person I was seeing was NOT my mother.
UNDERSTAND MY HOUSE HAVE ONE WOMAN, MY MOTHER. THAT-woman, MY MOTHER, NOT.

I continued to walk to the TV and after turning it off I look back down the hall and noticed the woman was now gone; I dismissed it since I was tired and ready for bed.
ANYWAY, TV I CL:1 walk to it, TURN O-F-F CL:1 walk down hall, WOMAN STILL THERE? Shake head, GONE. PSHAW, TIRED I, READY BED.

About a week later one of my brothers was in the kitchen sitting in my usual spot.
ABOUT 1 WEEK LATER HAPPEN MY BROTHER HE SIT WHERE? KITCHEN MY HABIT CHAIR.

I noticed that he had a machete leaning against the wall and I was curious to know why so pointing at the machete I asked, "Tye, what's up?"

I CL:1 walk towards him NOTICE THERE index WHAT? SWORD M-A-C-H-E-T-E SWORD. I CURIOUS, TAP++ HEY, SWORD INDEX-there FOR-FOR?

"Over the last two weeks I keep getting the feeling that someone else is in the house and I have seen someone in the living room."
(role shift) SINCE 2 WEEKS, AGAIN++ HAPPEN I FEEL GUT SOMEONE HERE IN HOUSE, I SOMETIMES SOMEONE SEE THERE-index LIVING ROOM THERE-index.

I began to feel goose bumps and as the hair on my neck raised, he continued,
HAPPEN I HAIR ON NECK STAND UP, WHY? HE STORY

"And I decided that if it ever comes for me, I have protection and if I swing and it don't fall, I can still use it to smash the window out and I can run!"
IF HAPPEN THAT SOMEONE COME-approach me I SWING KNIFE, HAPPEN IT DIE NOT? WINDOW, I BREAK, ESCAPE ME WILL!

I could tell from his expression that he was serious as a heart attack!
HIS EXPRESSION SERIOUS, MEAN STORY TRUE-BIZ

I began to wonder if I wanted to even bother watching my shows that night.
I MULL-OVER, T-V I WATCH SHOULD?

When Tye left me alone in the kitchen and he took his machete with him, I opted to turn in early.
BROTHER HE LEAVE. ME ALONE NOW! I DECIDE BED NOT T-V.

After a week or so of no laughs, I dismissed the thought of ghost and night visitors and I returned to my evening routine. I needed my fix of British comedy.
ONE WEEK, I NO T-V, NO LAUGH HA HA NONE! DECIDE T-V EVERY NIGHT MUST WATCH AGAIN MUST. GHOST

PSHAW, I IGNORE. T-V PROGRAM I MISS B-R-I-T-I-S-H FUNNY, I ADDICTED.

11:30 came quicker than usual or so it felt. I put my tea cup in the sink and threw away the napkin after putting the cookie bag in the cupboard and after turning the TV off, I saw her again!
THAT NIGHT I WATCH, TIME SEEM FAST 11:30 WOW! I CLEAN-UP, SINK I PUT CUP, COOKIE OPEN CUPBOARD put cookies in, NAPKIN THROW-AWAY, T-V TURN-OFF. SHOCKED, WOMAN AGAIN THERE I SEE AGAIN!

I don't remember if I even turned the kitchen lights off; I know I raced past the living room and dove in my bed and under the covers without looking back.
LIGHTS TURN-OFF? I DON'T REMEMBER. HAPPEN KITCHEN I ESCAPE, RUN STRAIGHT MY ROOM, ZOOM-GONE, BED THERE-INDEX JUMP-IN, COVERS OVER HEAD!

The next morning I spoke to my parents about the apparition that both Tye and I seemed to be plagued by. As my mother was making breakfast, I approached her first appealing to her motherly concern for the child's wellbeing.
MORNING, BREAKFAST MOM COOK, NEWSPAPER DAD READ. I DECIDE TALK THEM ABOUT GHOST MUST. TYE ME BOTH US SEE, MUST TELL. DECIDE MOM, I TELL HER, KNOW MOM TAKE CARE CHILDREN, I TELL HER.

"Mom, can we move?"
Tap tap mom, MOM WE MOVE CAN?

She did not respond. So I repeated my question, "Mom, can we move?"
MOM LOOK ME NOTHING, IGNORE? ASK AGAIN I. tap MOM, WE MOVE CAN?

"Boy hush."
SHUT UP

"No for real, I want to move. I think our house is haunted. Can we move please?"
MOM, TRUE I WANT MOVE. HOUSE HERE HAVE GHOST, WE MOVE PLEASE?

"You can move. Move your butt to the table and get ready to eat breakfast!"
FINE YOU MOVE CAN, MOVE THERE-index TABLE THERE SIT BREAKFAST EAT!

Hearing the shift in her voice and the colorful adjectives she added, which I have omitted from my retelling of my story, I decided it best to go sit down as I was instructed.
MOM HER EXPRESSION I NOTICE, ALSO SHE CURSE, FOR YOU I CHANGE, DELETE BAD WORD. ANYWAY, I DECIDE GOOD IDEA GO SIT.

I turned my attention to my dad. He had just finished reading the newspaper and was about to begin the crossword so I whispered so my mother would not hear me.
MY DAD CL:bent V sit there across from me. NEWSPAPER READ RECENTLY FINISH. C-R-O-S-S-W-O-R-D HE NOW READY DO. I WHISPER, MOM I HEAR ME I NOT WANT.

"Dad, can we move?"
Tap tap DAD, WE MOVE CAN?

"What, what did you say?"
SAY WHAT?

Increasing my volume a bit, "I said can we move?"
AGAIN I WHISPER, LITTLE LOUDER, WE MOVE CAN?

As my dad replied, my mother turned and gave me "The Look."
DAD RESPOND AND MOM HAVE EXPRESSION, I EEEEK

"Did you ask your mother?"
YOUR MOTHER, YOU ASK HER?

"Yeah and she told me to move my butt to the table."
Nod, YES SHE TELL ME TABLE SIT DOWN.

He laughed
DAD LAUGH

"Why do you want to move? You don't like this house?"
YOU WANT MOVE WHY? HOUSE HERE NOT LIKE?

"I think it's haunted."
HERE HAVE GHOST, I THINK YES.

"What?"
W-H-T (lexicalized "what")?!

I proceeded to explain the events that had transpired over the last three months; he sat patiently and listened before he spoke. My dad always did that before he gave his words of wisdom.
I STORY TELL UP TIL NOW 3 MONTHS WHOLE STORY INFORM HIM. HE PAY ATTENTION, PATIENT. STORY FINISH ME. DAD HIS TEND LISTEN, THINK THEN ANSWER.

"Well, I don't think moving is the best choice under the circumstances. This woman you and Tye seem to be seeing has not done anything to either of you and she has had ample time and opportunity so it would seem that she is not a malevolent spirit and therefore nothing to run from; in fact, you should invite her into the kitchen for some tea and cookies one night."
YOU STORY EXPLAIN, I UNDERSTAND BUT WE MOVE GOOD IDEA NOT. YOU, TYE TWO-YOU SEE WOMAN BUT SHE HURT YOU? NOT. IF WANT HURT YOU, SHE HAVE OPPORTUNITY. THINK SHE EVIL, I DON'T. MY PERSPECTIVE, YOU DO-DO? ONE NIGHT, INVITE HER SHARE TEA, COOKIE.

He then paused, smiled a bit and continued, "While you are at it, ask he for the lotto number for next week so we can hit the big million jackpot, ok?"

HE SMILE THEN SAY, ALSO KNOW LOTTO NUMBER, ASK HER TELL YOU. WE WIN CAN OK?

As my parents then laughed, I sulked and ate my bacon and eggs. MOM DAD TWO THEM LAUGH. BACON EGG I EAT, I MAD.

About a week later, there I was again laughing uncontrollably first at Benny Hill and then at Dave Allen. At 11:30 my laughter ceased. LATER ONE WEEK, KITCHEN I THERE BELLY LAUGH, ONE HOUR LAUGH, PROGRAM TWO FINISH TIME 11:30, I LAUGH FINISH.

I did my clean up and I turned the TV off and was about to dart upstairs again when I could hear my father's voice telling me to talk to the apparition. KITCHEN I CLEAN, T-V OFF, GO BED I READY BUT I REMEMBER FATHER HE TELL-ME SCARED NOT.

My parents were big on the face your fears philosophy and so I stood my ground and in the strongest trembling voice I could muster, I called to her. MY PARENTS TWO-THEM SUPPORT FEAR FACE FEAR FACE! I LEARN NOW DECIDE FACE! KITCHEN THERE MIDDLE I STAND, MY VOICE WEAK QUIET, I CALL GHOST.

"Hello, Miss. . . yooo hooo. In the living room, do you want some tea and cookies before I go to bed?" HELLO, WOMAN tap tap LIVING ROOM THERE, WANT COME-HERE TEA DRINK, COOKIES EAT WANT?

I closed my eyes fearing a gust of wind was soon to envelope me as a long haired wicked female spirit floated into the kitchen. To my relief, there was no wind and no evil sprit; however I still felt the need to confront this fear. MY EYES, I CLOSED. I TERRIFIED THOUGHT MAYBE GHOST LIKE WIND SURROUND ME, EVIL WOMAN HAIR LONG FLY

AROUND ME. I RELIEF, WHY? WIND NONE, EVIL GHOST NONE BUT FACE FEAR FINISH ME? NOT-YET.

I walked down the hall and into the living room. I stood in the middle of the room and looked at the chair, which was empty of course. I looked around the room. The entire room was still and quiet. As I turned to see my reflection in the huge wall mirror opposite the door and the chair, I noticed that someone was sitting in the chair and she was beginning to stand up.

HALL I CL:1 walk, LIVING ROOM I INTO. ROOM MIDDLE I STAND, CHAIR THERE-index GHOST THERE? NOTHING EMPTY. ROOM I LOOK AROUND. ROOM ALL QUIET, GHOST NONE. LIVING ROOM HAVE WALL, THERE HAVE MIRROR CL:1-1 LARGE. I LOOK, MIRROR SEE MYSELF THERE-index LOOK AROUND SHOCKED! WHY? MIRROR THERE I SEE CHAIR EMPTY STILL? NO! WOMAN THERE SIT!

Now I could tell you that I was scared, but scared and terrified don't seem to come close to what I was feeling as I stood motionless watching her in the mirror's reflection stand and begin to approach me. Looking at her in the mirror, she was now standing about six feet from me. Some how, I found the courage to turn around. Thankfully, she was not there. I am sure I would have urinated in my pants if she had been.

ME SCARED? NOT, I COULD TELL YOU BUT SCARED TERRIFIED NOT ENOUGH, FEEL WOW SCARED AWFUL. I STAND FROOZE LOOK MIRROR. WOMAN THERE SIT STAND WALK, APPROACH ME. REMEMBER I LOOK MIRROR SEE HAPPEN, I BRAVE FEAR FACE MUST, I TURN AROUND.

WOMAN THERE? NO. LUCKY ME. IF TURN AROUND SEE WOMAN THERE SAME LIKE MIRROR, HAPPEN I P-E-E TRUE-BIZ.

The old saying curiosity killed the cat never really applied to me until now because what I SHOULD have done was leave the room and go to bed.

KNOW OLD QUOTE HAPPEN CAT DIE WHY CURIOUS
NOSY WELL ME SAME CURIOUS. GO BED I SHOULD BUT
GO? NOT

What I DID was turn back to look in the mirror again and sure enough,
clear as day, she was standing there. This time she was even closer and
was beginning to raise her hand to touch my shoulder.
I DO-DO? TURN LOOK MIRROR AGAIN. WOW, WOMAN
THERE! STAND FAR ME? NO. NOW CLOSE!

Again I turned, praying that again she would not be there but she
was there! She was not a reflection this time, she was a five foot, pale
skinned, translucent woman wearing a long wedding like gown, deep
blue eyes and bright red lips, and she was about to touch my shoulder!
I PRAY HAPPEN I TURN AROUND AND NOTHING BUT I
TURN AND WOMAN THERE STAND SAME MIRROR STAND
CLOSE ME! WOMAN SHORT FIVE F-T, PALE SEE THROUGH
VAGUE. CLOTHES WHAT? WEDDING DRESS. HER EYES
BLUE STRONG, LIPS RED STRONG. WOMAN THERE CLOSE
ME, SHE DO-DO? REACH

Now, please don't go telling anyone this, cause it is embarrassing enough
to tell you but I did in fact pee all over myself and half the floor probably
as I ran through her, out the house where I cowered in a corner on the
front porch until I felt my mother's swift hand slapping my upside the
head that next morning, telling me to get in the house and get washed
up!
O-K, O-K PLEASE SECRET, GO GOSSIP NO, I EMBARRASS
ALREADY BUT I P-E-E TRUE-BIZ! P-E-E ME, FLOOR. HAPPEN
I ESCAPE, RUN! HOUSE I LEAVE SLEEP OUTSIDE WHERE?
P-O-R-C-H. MORNING, MOM FIND, SLAP ME. SHE TELL ME
GO, IN house, WASH, GO!

No one has seen the woman since but to this day foot steps can be heard
pacing in the attic, which as I found out from doing some research at
the library, was where the daughter of the previous owner committed
suicide on her wedding day when her fiancée left town with a maid of
honor.

THAT EXPERIENCE SINCE WOMAN APPEAR AGAIN NOT BUT HEAR HER THERE-index up A-T-T-I-C WALK. HAPPEN I GO LIBRARY RESEARCH FIND STORY ABOUT WOMAN KILL SELF WHY? HER WEDDING FIANCEE AND M-A-I-D-O-F-H-O-N-O-R TWO-THEM LEAVE TOGETHER.

Let's look and see what you came up with.

Characters: Storyteller/narrator – me, Tye the brother, mother, father, and the female ghost. Other people mentioned are Benny Hill and Dave Allen, ghost's father, her fiancée and maid of honor. They are not characters, but are people mentioned in the story that still need to be set up in some way.

Time: We are looking back at a situation that occurred in the late '70s or early '80s. The story took place over several weeks. The story predominately occurs at night between the hours of 10:30 and 11:30, but there are two early morning references.

Setting: My family home, kitchen, hallway, bedroom, living room, front porch, and the attic. Other places mentioned that you may or may not actually show would be the library, place of her wedding, and from where the fiancée is leaving.

Summary of situation: Several nights of seeing a ghost and the eventual confrontation with the specter.

CLASSIFIERS

The use of classifiers is one major way to show something versus telling it. Classifier use is an integral part of ASL, in general—not only in ASL performing and interpreting, but in conversational ASL as well. If you do not currently use classifiers, you may want to start finding out more about them—and how to use them—so that you can incorporate them into your conversation skills, interpreting, and/or your performing. Let's start with:

What are classifiers?
Classifiers are specific handshapes used in several grammatical ways.

Classifiers act as adjectives when they show how something looks by indicating size and shape of an object.

Classifiers act as verbs to show how something moves or is moved in a directional manner.

Classifiers act as nouns and pronouns.

Classifiers also indicate location and spatial relationship of two or more objects.

There are many ways to be creative and "show" what you are talking about. Rather than tell about a traffic incident, can you creatively show the scene? I have seen the "Star Spangled Banner" signed very flat without classifiers, and I have seen it signed with many of them. One place in the song is when the flag, itself, is spoken about. I have seen the bent L classifier used to indicate the stripes and the bent 5 handshape (claw) used to show the stars on the flag. That is much more visual than simply signing *flag*, wouldn't you agree?

Think about story A again (or any song), and find what in the story (or song) can be set up and shown using classifiers. Remember that, in many ways, your song is a story; so go through the storytelling steps and break it down—as we have previously—by identifying time, place, events, and characters. Make the two-dimensional story come alive in 3-D.

Here are some of the more common classifiers:

CL:1
Can represent a pencil, a leg, or a person standing upright.

CL: bent 5
Can represent an object in a certain location (i.e., a house or a school).

CL:3
Can represent vehicles (i.e., a bicycle, motorcycle, or one or more cars).

CL:B
Can represent flat things such as an elevator door, a map, a bridge, or can also be a car.

CL:C
Can represent small, round, thick objects such as a cup, can, or candle.

CL:CC
Can represent larger round, thick objects such as a tree, lamppost, column in front of a museum, or a garbage can.

CL:F
Can represent small, round items such as a piece of jewelry, a button, coin, or a pepperoni.

CL:FF
Can be used to represent someone's eyes looking around at something.

CL:V

When used in the upside-down "V" position, this can represent a person standing upright, a person's legs, or a person walking, jumping, skipping, etc. When in the "V" position, it can represent two people walking. This classifier can also be used to represent someone's eyes looking around.

It is important to remember that classifiers are not actual signs; they are used to represent "classes" of things / general categories. Many beginners mistakenly believe they are signs; again, I repeat they are not actual signs for a word. For example, CL:3 is not the sign for car; it is a classifier that can be used to represent a car, bike, motorcycle, or jet ski. They can be used to describe the appearance (size and shape) of an object or person.

I want the shirt with *vertical stripes*. (You could use the CL:4 to indicate the stripes.)

They can be used to represent the object or person itself, or the way the object moves or relates to other objects (or people.)

Mary just *ran by* us without speaking. (You could use CL:1 to indicate Mary and the fast manner in which she zipped by.)

See the car *there*? My car is the one behind it. (You could use CL:3 to indicate the car locations in relation to one another.)

If you remember this, you are well on your way to making a more visually pleasing product.

The classifiers represented here are a tiny sampling of what is possible.

• Descriptive Classifiers (DCL) are also known as size and shape specifiers (SASSes). They describe a person or object.

DCL:B (or bent B) "extremely tall" [Explanation: to represent the descriptive classifier "extremely tall," you hold the "bent 'B' hand" high in the air while using an appropriate facial expression.]

DCL:B (or bent B) "short"
DCL:4 "long hair"
DCL:1 "bulletin board"
DCL:1 "black board"
DCL:4 (claw) "freckles"
DCL:4 "striped"
DCL:G "thin"
DCL:4 (claw) "curly hair"

- Semantic Classifiers represent categories of nouns (i.e., people or vehicles)

SCL:1 (person) "walking fast"
SCL:1 (person) "person walks to..._____"
SCL:3 (car) "drives to_____"
SCL:Y (fat person) "waddling"
SCL:flattened-O (fast-car) "cruising"
SCL:bent-V (row of chairs)

- Locative Classifiers show placement or spatial information about an object. These sometimes indicate movement.

LCL:C/LCL:B "place cup on napkin"
LCL:5 "leaf floating to the ground"
LCL:1 (sticks) "one here-one here"
LCL:B "shelf" (over to the right)
LCL:1 "goal-posts"
(2h)LCL:L "adjust a picture"

- Plural Classifiers indicates a specific number or a non-specific number.

PCL:2 "two people walking"
PCL:4 "long line of people"
PCL:4 "people moving in line"
PCL: 5 "hordes of _____." (Often called "scads of")
PCL:V "people seated in a circle"

• Instrument Classifiers use your hands (or another part of your body) to manipulate an "object."

ICL "driving"
ICL "hammer in a nail"
ICL "play checkers"
ICL "play chess"
ICL "light match"
ICL (broom) ICL "sweep"
ICL (water) ICL "pour in"
ICL (garbage) ICL "dump out"
ICL (wash clothes) ICL "hang up"

• Body Classifiers/Mime
You use your body to "act out" or "role play." Sometimes this is like "miming. " Other times, you show the action (or interaction) that is going on. This often involves "role shifting."

"yawn"
"acting tough"
"give a hug to a child"
"running hard/pumping arms"
"wave to crowd"
"listen for strange noise"

• Bodypart Classifiers
A specific part of your body is doing an action.

BPCL:F(2h) - representing the eyes looking at something
BPCL:1 - index fingers representing legs, crossing legs
BPCL:B - representing the foot as in tapping foot
BPCL:S (fist) representing the head of a person

Classifier Predicates:
A classifier (in ASL) is a sign that represents a general category of things, shapes, or sizes.

A predicate is the part of a sentence that modifies (says something about or describes) the topic of the sentence or some other noun or noun phrase in the sentence. (Valli & Lucas, 2000)

Example: JOHN HANDSOME
The topic is "John." Handsome is an "adjective predicate" describing John's appearance.

Example: JOHN RUN
The topic is "John." Run is a "verb predicate" stating what John did or is doing.

Example: JOHN BED
The topic is "John." Bed is a "noun predicate" stating John's location.

Example: JOHN CL:FF "eyes quickly looked at right"
The topic is "John." CL:FF represents a "classifier predicate" indicating that John quickly looked to his right.

Whenever you use a classifier to describe the shape, size, movement, or location of a noun, you are using a "classifier predicate."

[Segments used with permission from Dr. Vicars of ASL University]

MOUTHING MORPHEMES

Mouthing morphemes are another one of those inseparable parts of ASL grammar. The use of non-manual signals must be incorporated for the sentences to grammatically make sense. Your eyebrows and facial expressions contain vital bits of grammatical information, and therefore are very important to the use of the language. They are also very important in your performance style. Your songs (stories) should incorporate the use of mouthing morphemes and non-manual signals if for no other reason than to present a fluent and linguistically accurate presentation.

Examples of some mouthing morphemes are:

CHA – Size: Height, Weight, Length, Quantity
That man is (CHA) tall.
I have (CHA) work to do.
The auditorium is (CHA) large.

PUCKERED LIPS with awful sign – Terrific, Wow, Interesting
Ann Rice is a (PUCKERED LIPS with awful sign) phenomenal author.
That movie was really (PUCKERED LIPS with awful sign) interesting.
(PUCKERED LIPS with awful sign) WOW! You got the new X-Box 16!

FISH – Finished, Done, Stop it
Is your homework (FISH) done?
(FISH) Stop bothering your sister.

TH – Clumsy, Lousy, Careless
I tried to read the letter but his (TH) handwriting was hard to read.
When you drink, you know you (TH) can't walk.
I saw his new movie and it was (TH) lousy.

PUFFED (Cheeks) – Very fat, Long ago, Many
That room has (PUFFED) many seats.
(PUFFED) Long ago, our family lived in Ireland.
His dog is (PUFFED) fat.

STA-STA – Struggle, Long process, Over and over again
You and your boss have been (STA-STA) working on that project for a year now.
My fiancée and I (STA-STA) struggled with our decision to rent or buy a condo.
Pastor John's message is the (STA-STA) same as always.

LICK [THUP] – Swallow, Tired of, Run out, All gone
All of the milk is (THUP) gone.
We (THUP) ran out of tickets at noon.

I have seen may people perform songs and, as they are signing, (English word order) they also mouth each and every word of the song (lip-syncing.) That is transliteration and is not the goal we are aiming for in this text. That skill and application has its place. Our goal is performing the most idiomatic ASL translation possible, which means incorporating mouthing morphemes—not lip-syncing every word. Yes, an occasional English word on the lips is effective; however, every word is not. We are ultimately striving to utilize mouthing morphemes, as they are appropriate in the song, and in daily conversational and interpreting use. Many find this ASL method much more challenging because you are signing and mouthing things that many times are not close to the English words being sung or spoken. Yes, it is challenging and often times difficult, but is part of the process and I guarantee you that it is a journey well worth the time and effort you are investing. Your overall ASL skills will greatly improve as you master this and the other skills suggested.

Visual Vernacular

Are you familiar with this term – visual vernacular? The first time I came across that term was in "Lessons in Laughter," which is the title of an autobiographical book and video of and interview with acclaimed Deaf actor Bernard Bragg. On the video, he first explains what the term means and then he demonstrates it. His demonstration is quite fascinating because he demonstrates one story about war bombers blowing up a town and the second about a pilot and an eagle. His demonstrations are done without focusing on specific words. He utilizes handshapes, classifiers, body language, and facial expression, to tell a story... and yet he really does not tell the story – he SHOWS the story! To put in my own words - Visual Vernacular is described as making the story (song) visual in a cinematographic manner. It is dramatizing it and making it more like watching a movie. Also like a movie, visual vernacular shows the scene in several ways by incorporating:

Distance – am I seeing it close up, mid range, long range / panoramic view or zooming? It shows various perspectives or vantage points as the characters shift. Think of the movie "Superman Returns" as one possible example. There is a scene when a bank robber shoots Superman in the eye with a bullet. That is an extreme close up (or zoomed in) shot of the bullet smashing against his eye and we also, for added effect, see it happen in slow motion.

Timing / Speed – am I seeing something happen in regular speed, faster than normal speed, or in slow motion? Think of the "Matrix" where super slow motion was used to heighten the effect of Neo evading bullets at super speed.

Vantage point – am I seeing it from character A's perspective or character B's? How does role shifting show perspective and point of view? Think of the movie "Silence of the Lambs" where we see two views of where Dr. Lector is held. We see his cell from two views. One is from the view of agent Starling looking in on Lector the prisoner. View two from that of Dr. Lector looking through the glass at agent Starling. Another example is King Kong, where we see the perspective of the pilots shooting at Kong, the woman not wanting him to be shot, and of Kong being shot.

On the video, Mr. Bragg says, "Deaf people make excellent filmmakers because they already think and speak visually, like a movie."

As you begin to develop your visual vernacular and directorial skills, keep these elements in mind:

Distance:
How close or far do I want to show the scene? How can I alternate between close, mid, far, panorama, or zooming in? Why am I showing it from that distance? How is that enhancing the story?

Timing/Speed:
How fast or slow do I want to show the scene? Why am I showing it at that speed? How is that enhancing the story?

Vantage point/Point of view:
Whose view am I seeing? How do I switch to show different views, different emotions, and perspectives of the same event, conversations and interactions between people? Why am I showing it from that vantage point? How is that enhancing the story?

Take a minute to pop your favorite film into the DVD player and notice how—as the film begins - the camera angles change, and how some things may change in tempo and speed, distance, and even sound. This is what we are working to emulate in ASL Visual Vernacular.

One of my favorite films to observe is the "Matrix." I am still entranced by the use of angles, speed, slow motion, and point of view, etc.
Let's also take a moment to analyze Austin's "Deaf Ninja" story that I mentioned earlier, but let's do so in light of Visual Vernacular.
The following translation was posted online as an example of **one** person's translation.

:05 - :16. You know what one of my constant challenges is? With everything happening out there in the real world, I find myself daydreaming to the point where I completely get submerged in my own visionary, all by my isolated self. That's just me, who I am [clapping self on chest]. *Overall, his tone is calm and non-apologetic (which is seen by his facial expressions and the way he slightly lifts his shoulders). (You see him signing "isolate" – index finger to temple, then "I's" meeting together)*

:17. Let me give you an example.

(The way he brings his hands together is a natural way of telling us that he's taking a dramatic pause.)

:18 – :22. I remember how, a long time ago, when I was a young kid, my older, deaf brother *(pointing a finger away from his self indicates to the audience that he is talking about a passive object, his brother.)*

:23 – :26. He wore one of those old-fashioned hearing aids – don't you remember those? *(You will see the sign for "know", but in this context, it can also be used for "recall/remember") (uses his scrunched eyebrows to kind of confirm with the audience that they understand what he means.)*

:26 – :27. They came with this gigantic box worn on the chest *(he uses his facial expressions to exaggerate the size of the box and also spreads out his hands and clenches it to his chest, to really emphasize how big the hearing aid box was. This invariably brings out a chuckle to many of us deaf users, because we recall too well how big these boxes were and how we unfortunately had to wear them on our chests.)*

:27 – :30. A cord/rope hung around the neck to support the box. And then these two cords, connected to the sides of the box, went straight to the ears. With all of this set-up, one had no choice but to just strut around as if he were The Man. *(He's using a lot of facial expressions to sort of mock the use of this box, especially its awkward design. See if you can identify them)*

:31 – :32. I'd take a look at him and snicker. But then suddenly, I was caught off guard.

:33 – :35. My brother, as he'd so often does, took the cord and ear pieces out of his ears. He did this in a menacing and plotting behavior *(look at his eyebrows and eyes, open mouth.)*

:36 – :39. Holding the cord ends by both hands, my brother used them to swing them defensively/aggressively

:40 – :41. I had to literally fend off his swings *(note how he uses his facial expressions to tell half of the story here. Here, you can see that it was a clear challenge, hence my insert of "literally" even though the guy did not sign this word. He said it all in his face). Also note the way he shifts his body to show who is doing the swing, and then who is receiving the swipes. This is how you convey point of perspective character shifts.*

:42 – :43. Eh *(the way he holds up his right hand and changes his face instantly breaks the story-telling mode, telling us that segment was over. He does this in a neutral way, by holding up his right hand).*

:44 – :48. So, one particular time, as I was fending off my brother's swings, a thought/vision suddenly struck me. *(See how he is powerful in the way he signs "rock hit index finger" – it indicates how rapid and strong that thought came to him (the index finger is a frequent classifier for self. Also observe how his facial expressions change the mood from that to the segue of his vision.)*

:49 – :51. Deaf. Ninja!

:52 – :54. It's night-time and very dark *(notice how he squints his eyes to emphasize this.)*

:55 – :58. The moon was covered by clouds moving past in their typical circular motion. *(Austin kind of "paints" this scene with his fingers in various positions of his hands. He also raises his eyebrows to convey how this stood out.)*

:59 – 1:01. This is kind of difficult to translate. He's then going on to describe the scene (*see how he moves his arms from the moon "up there" and then crosses his arms a few times to demonstrate perhaps the magnitude of the setting. He does not really tell us if it's land, water, or whatever. He leaves it up to us to imagine, but we feel as if we know exactly what he's talking about.*)

1:02 – 1:04. Now we see a face, all but the eyes covered by a mask. Those eyes are downright serious (*great tone here.*) That mask continues to engulf the entire body... in black. (*Note the way he slowly signs black... it adds more to the drama.*)

1:05 – 1:08. Again, we see Austin describing the hearing aid machine, accompanied by its cord. However, he adds the fact that it's glimmering (can you identify that sign?)

1:09 – 1:10. There's no exact English phrase to replace Austin's signing. At first, he animatedly waves his arms about to briefly break away from all the object-describing mode (moon, costume, hearing aid, mood.) The way he rotates his head to follow the hand farthest out tells us that he's able to observe/scan whatever's out in front of him, albeit in a guarded way (which the hand closes to him indicates – see how he holds both hands outward, as if ready to fight.)

1:11 – 1:12. Those eyes again. The Ninja's looking out and then moving around. (*He's using "L-shapes" to convey the eyelids being held slightly open, as in a cautious manner. And his eyebrows to show just how well he damn means business. Note how, as he twirls around, those eyelids of his also move along, they're an appendage of his and act as his "puppets".*)

1:13. Notice how he widens his eyes in a 'hey, you!' Manner – uncharacteristic of the Ninja, so we immediately know that he's no longer telling the story from the character's point of view and now shifting into a different point-of-view. He is now describing the environment.

1:14. It's starting to rain (note the guy's wide eyes), and then see how he slowly starts to minimize his "raining" hands <u>and</u> closes his eyes halfway

– the slow and short movements show that the rain is continuing and that it's now fading to just being part of the background.

1:14/5 – 1:16. Back to the character we go. Again using his "L" hand, we see that the Ninja notices something, far away (see how he uses his index finger to "flicker" – indicating how far away that is.)

1:16 – 1:17. What the Ninja notices is a water drop (or raindrop) falling from the sky.

1:18 – 1:20. Now squinting his eyes in a "ah, here we go" motif, and moving around to look in a different direction, see how his eyes widen and body starts to stand up a bit. He's spotted something - we know something is about to happen!

1:20. Enemy! Enemies! (See how he signs it once, and then repeatedly. This tells us that there's more than one enemy in a single sign, rather than signing "many enemies".)

1:21 – 1:22. I'm completely surrounded by these enemies coming toward me by the masses. *(He uses all of his fingers to show that there are many of them coming... these fingers represent the enemies coming. Note how his eyes seem "shocked" when he says enemy).* They're marching toward me *(note how he opens/closes his mouth to show their sinister marching.)* You can also obviously tell how he's feeling – quite something fierce, and getting ready to fight!

1:23. – Note how he moves all these "fingers" to convey a different angle of view. Instead of looking at the Ninja from one particular vantage of point, we're now looking at him from a different angle. And he goes on to describe just how big these enemies are. He scrunches up his face to really, really emphasize how huge they are – especially in the chest/arms!

1:25 – 1:27. These enemies have wood weapons (swords?) He signs "wood", and then uses a classifier to show the bad person drawing out the "wood" from a container, and that the bag is worn on the back (he visibly acts this out by pulling the sword out from behind his back.)

1:28. The enemy uses his weapon to strike out at the Ninja (note how Austin uses his body pose so we know that he's talking about the bad guy.)

1:29. Amidst the momentum, after some lashing out, the bad guy positions his knife upright, ever the more ready to continue fighting (use of facial expressions, mouth, arm movement to indicate this.)

1:30 – 1:34. There's also knives as well, worn on either side of the waist. They're huge! Austin uses his hands to indicate just how wide these blades are, and his face to further emphasize just how nasty these knives are.

1:34 – 1:35. We continue to see the bad guy fight with these knives.

1:36 – 1:38. Austin uses these two hands to tell us that this same description fits from the first enemy to the next enemy standing to him, and so on (the point is, all the enemies look and act the same.)

1:39 – 1:41. We're taken back to the Deaf Ninja, in his characteristic observing/scanning manner. He barely breaks a sweat as he takes in his environment full of hostile enemies.

1:41 – 1:43. Ah-ha! We now see the Deaf Ninja pull out his hearing aids and swing them about!

1:44. The Deaf Ninja is jumping high from the ground and circling around above ground (*you can see that it's high, by the way Austin opens his mouth wide.*)

1:46 – 1:48. You see Austin flipping his hands over - that bottom hand is still representing the ground, but we are now in a different phase of the story (even if just half a second later.) The Deaf Ninja is now not just jumping, but using his extended leg to really let it go at all the enemies surrounding him.

1:49 – 1:52. As the Deaf Ninja continues to hit his targets right-on target, he also continues to move around in a circular motion. We can see this by the way Austin spins his arms around. We also see the "heads" being knocked back, and then the "bodies" falling down. Austin is doing this repetitively, indicating that just about all of those soldiers are indeed falling down from his leg ninja act.

1:53 – 1:58. As the bodies continue to fall, the Deaf Ninja uses his ear-hearing cords to strike out at the faces of the remaining enemies. The hearing-aid cords cut right across their faces, and you can see Austin showing the blood spurting out from their faces.

1:59 – 2:02. Bodies are still falling. Note how Austin now signs those bodies in a different location, indicating that we're coming around the circle. When he points his index fingers downward and signs circle, he's indicating that this is going around the circle.

2:02 – 2:06. We see a majestic display of how all the enemies fall at once. They fall really hard. See how Austin "bounces" his hands to represent that.

2:06. We now see the Deaf Ninja landing on the ground from his mid-air combat.

2:07 – 2:08. We now see the Deaf Ninja catch his balance *(note Austin's use of clawed hands as to "steady the feet on the ground")*, still wearing his mask. Also note how Austin exhales – it's all over!

2:09 – 2:11. The Deaf Ninja has one last, furious bout of cord-swinging before he puts back in his ear-pieces. You see how his eyelids relax, also conveying his relaxed mode.

2:12 – 2:14. The Deaf Ninja half-way closes his eyes, swings them around in a different direction. Note how he opens them again – we know he's noticed something, or that his mood's changed.

2:15 – 2:17. The raindrop is STILL falling! Austin is signing this, and the way he squints his eyes indicates that the raindrop is far from where he is standing.

2:18. All of a sudden, the view of the raindrop changes so that it's no longer far away at the Deaf Ninja's side. We're now directly facing the rain drop, close to our faces.

2:19 – 2:22. Note how relaxed Austin is as he shows the raindrop slowly falling and splish-splashing, creating a ripple of water around its landing.

2:23. We're now taken back to the Ninja, who is now looking downward at the fallen raindrop in his classic observant behavior. But ah-ha – those index fingers move upward in an "X" position. They represent his eyebrows. He's clearly puzzled by something.

2:24 – 2:28. Oh, it's the hearing-aid box still on his chest. He's now struggling to listen and realizes he can't hear anything through the box/ hearing aids. "I can't hear. What's up with that?"

2:30 – 2:32. Austin shows himself being snapped awake by the reality of that hearing aid moment, and how the dream "closes". Austin blinks his eyes and goes "huh?"

2:32 – 2:39. Austin looks around, and sees his brother fumbling with the hearing aid box and cords, and then looking at Austin and going "I can't hear". *(Note how this is identical to what Austin just signed a moment ago, only now it's his deaf brother struggling.)*

2:39 – 2:41. Austin looks at his brother, and then looks at us from the side of his eyes. That says it all – whoa.

ACTING TECHNIQUES & STORYTELLING SKILLS

Acting can be a huge asset to the ASL performer and interpreter in that acting is a visual tool that can assist you in showing and becoming the character of a song or story. Acting gives you greater range to that painting palette I always mention so that you have greater options to pull from for your performances. You are not limited to one or two possible options. Your limit becomes the range of your imagination!

Remember that the root of acting is "Act" and to act means to do. . . What are you DOING? The audience does not know what you are feeling (unless my favorite "magician" artist Criss Angel is there and uses his "psychic" abilities and tells them.) The good or effective actor / performer tells the audience what he / she feels by what he / she does! It is in the doing that we not only see the feeling, but will feel empathy with the performer. We will cry when Sally Fields cries in "Steel Magnolias," not because we can feel her pain, but because we can see how distraught she "feels" by how she walks, talks, cries, and gestures. All of that moves us to tears because we can better identify with those visually identifiable signals for pain and grief.

You cannot act grief. You cannot act sad. What you can do is show what a sad person does – show how a sad person would walk, talk, and drink coffee. You can show what a grief-stricken person does – how he / she answers the phone, opens his / her mail, and cooks dinner.

As the ASL performer, think about (and carefully select) what you can DO to become the character of the song, to convey the emotion of the song. If the singer (character) is mad, what can you do to show that he is angry? To help you identify if you are on the right track, ask yourself: If I were to stop signing, would the audience still know that I as the character am angry? How would they know what I am feeling? What am I doing to show that? When I perform the song **"Watch the**

Lamb", can you see any emotion based on my facial expression, body language and mannerisms? It is through the doing that you sense the feeling.

What makes a movie a "good" movie? What does it take for you to become engrossed in the movie (which, as we know, is nothing more than a story?) What makes one story better than another story? What makes one a better storyteller than another? Do you know someone who people love to hear tell stories? What is it about them or their abilities that make them the preferred storyteller at work or in the family? What makes one actor your favorite, and another your least favorite? Some actors make you forget they are acting or that you are watching a movie, while others are so obviously acting that you can't wait until it's over.

Let's look at a few things that are important to the story. Some of this is a recap from a few sections before. Repetition never hurts and some of this acting stuff will be mentioned again later, so take note.

"Practice doesn't make perfect; but it most certainly makes better and permanent."

At the center of ALL stories are the characters. Who are the characters the story is about? Without the characters, there is no story. Now to build on that concept, you need something to happen to the characters. You need drama or, more specifically, you need conflict. It is the conflict that makes the story interesting, entertaining, and effective. The audience must be interested in the character's drama, the journey the character must go through and the conflict faced. If I don't care about the character(s), I won't care about the story.

Becoming the character of the song/story
Who are the characters in the song? What are the characters doing, feeling, and saying and to whom are they singing? Once you can answer those questions, you can begin to dramatize the character and song. Show me—don't tell me—the song. Think about the mannerisms of the character in the song (not the actual singer) and adopt some of those mannerisms for your performance.

CHARACTER DEVELOPMENT

Who is in the story and who is the story about? Who is the "star" of the story? The protagonist has a goal or mission; what is it? Who is preventing that goal or mission from being accomplished (the antagonist?) Who are the co-stars and what is their significance in the story? No one is ever there "just because." Even the "extras" in a movie serve a purpose.

Once you are clear and know who they all are, why they all are there, what they all want, and what they are all doing, you can develop more about them in terms of developing their appearances and mannerisms as you move to the visual version.

What do they look like, how do they behave, how do they walk and talk (sign), etc.? Be very clear so you can "become" the characters of the story as you present it.

Let's revisit Goldilocks.

How does Papa Bear look, how does he stand, how does he move, how does he (speak) sign? How is Papa Bear different in relation to Mama, Baby, and Goldilocks? Each of them should have a very distinct and visually identifiable look and style.

Are you wondering, again, what this has to do with performing a song?

Isn't a song in many ways a mini story? It is always about someone or something, right? And something is happening, hummm?

All of the things I have talked to you about – classifiers, visual vernacular, mouthing morphemes, etc. are all directly related to your song presentation. If your goal is to increase your ASL performance style, your ASL conversation style, or your ASL interpreting style, then this storytelling information is important and applicable to your goals. A proficient ASL conversationalist incorporates many of the tools I have mentioned here just as the skilled interpreter and performer utilized them.

In order to improve your storytelling skills, I suggest that certain acting technique be incorporated into your repertoire.

What is Acting?

Acting is doing; it is to act or to do something. Acting is not about feeling the "feelings" because feelings are internal and invisible to the audience. It is not "being" mad or "being" sad. If the character is happy, depressed or angry, how does the audience know it? We know because we see how the character "acts"; we see what he or she is doing, how they are behaving, their mannerisms, facial expressions, tone when speaking, and all that they are "showing" us. The actor is "showing" the audience what the character feels by demonstration - by what the character is "doing."

In order to become a separate character in the song/story, you have to demonstrate that character in a manner that is convincing. It is not "you" who is eating porridge, it is not you dodging bullets, it is not you fighting Darth Vadar; you are becoming the character and showing how that character is acting in that given situation in the story (song.)

While there are several ways to do that, they are all connected to "acting." Just as the artist learns to master the use of canvas, paint, brush or hammer and chisel, you must develop the use of your tools. Skillful mastery of the following will greatly influence how effectively you are portraying the characters of the story/song:

Your face
Your body
Your use of language (your signing)

Your Face

Looking in a mirror, experiment with your facial expressions. One of the first exercises is to show a variety of moods / emotions on your face.

What does happy "look like" on your face? Sadness, joy, depression, fear, excitement, anxiety, boredom . . .?

You will notice that many of them can be very similar. For example, fear and shock or surprise may look similar on your face. Is there a way you can make each more distinct? Is there a way to alter them so that fear and surprise do not look alike or boredom and depression do not look alike? It is a good thing that the face works in conjunction with the body because what you do in association to how you look will more clearly identify the mood, emotion, and feeling you are portraying. Controlling your face is the first stage in acting the part of the character. Isn't it interesting that your face is also vitally important in terms of ASL grammatical fluency?

Your Body

You will again be using your best friend—the mirror—as you now experiment with your body movements. How do "you" move? One thing I spent a lot of time learning and doing, while I was a graduate theatre student at Virginia Commonwealth University, was learning to observe how "I" move and do things. Most people never truly observe—and are rarely conscious of—their own idiosyncrasies, habits, traits, or mannerisms. To help become aware of yours, become mindful of how you move. How do you walk? How do you drink? Do you always open doors by reaching with the same hand? Do you blow your coffee or sip first? Become a student of you. Watch and become aware of your instrument. In addition to studying "you", it is also helpful to "people watch." In fact, you may want to observe them first. Often times—by seeing what others are doing or saying—you open the door to your own awareness as you see yourself in them, in either similarities or dissimilarities. Observe how other people do simple everyday activities. How do people walk, pick up a cup, open a door, sit in a chair or stand up? Do you notice any things people do repeatedly like quirks, biting nails, tapping the table, pushing hair out of the face, or rubbing eyes? Having seen what other people do, it often opens the eyes of the observer to what he / she does. Once you know your movement patterns, you can more effectively make choices to create a character's movement patterns. How does that character stand, walk, and hold a cup? How is that different, not only from you, but from other characters as well?

Your use of language / Your Signing

Each person has a distinct signing style, just as each person has a distinct speaking style and writing style. Some people speak clearly and enunciate each word, while others blur words and phrases together. Some people speak loud and forceful, while others are quiet and timid. Signing is the same. Some sign clear and others do not. Some sign big and others sign small. What is your style? Observe your own traits and characteristics when you sign. If possible, and I encourage you to make it possible, videotape yourself telling several stories, interpreting something, or just having a mock conversation. Identify things you tend to do that are trademarks of your style – your idiosyncrasies. You can also ask someone in the Deaf community who is skilled and fluent to give you feedback on your style. I have also learned that it is always a good idea to keep the parameters of ASL in mind. If you are conscious of them in respect to how you sign, you will be more able to critique yourself effectively more often.

Quick reminder of the parameters:

Handshape: What is the shape of your hand?
Example - a "5" handshape as used in the sign for Mother.

Location: Where is the sign located?
Example – a "5" handshape at the chin is "mother," but at the forehead is "father."

Movement: How does the sign move?
Example – a "5" handshape at the chin is "mother," but if the hand moves forward it becomes "grandmother."

Palm Orientation: Where is the palm of your hand facing?
Example – with the sign for "sit" or "chair", your palms are facing the ground, but for the sign "name", your palms are facing inwards toward your body.

Non-manual: What happens on your face and body versus the actual signs.
Example – Moving the eyebrows in the correct manner to signify a Yes/No question or a "Wh" question; also mouthing morphemes.

Once you have identified "your" style, you can then address the next question. How do each of the characters in the story/song sign? How can you sign in a way so each character's signing is different from the others?

Unless the character is supposed to purposely be unclear and unintelligible (such as in the animated series "Fat Albert"—the character Mush Mouth, or the adults on the "Charlie Brown" cartoons, and Kenny in "South Park"), you want the audience to understand what is being said. So make sure to be clear, sign large, and produce the signs effectively—even if the character signs lazily, you want to be clear as a lazy person.

ASL Poetry

Another very creative use of ASL is the art form of ASL poetry. ASL poetry does not rely on the auditory or even the written parameters of poetics. ASL poetry is visual in nature and execution. There are several features of ASL poetry that we can incorporate into our storytelling and song presentations.

Handshape – Using similar or carefully selected handshapes for creative emphasis and meaning in the poem.
An example would be signing the following gloss using a "B" handshape for all five signs: OUR GOD YOU IN HEAVEN.

Sign Variations – Using several signs that have a similar meaning. For example: GO. Depending on what you are saying, there are several ways you could sign the meaning GO. When using poetics, awareness of this is very useful.

Altering a Sign – There are times when it is acceptable to alter a sign for creative impact and meaning. One example that first comes to my mind is altering the sign for LORD, when referring to Jesus as Lord or God. Typically, it is signed: Using the right hand "L" (if right-handed) and moving it from the left shoulder to the right hip. Alternate: Using the right hand "L" and moving it from the left shoulder to upper area where you would sign God.

Duration of the Movement – The speed at which you produce the signs is also important in ASL poetry. Alternating between fast and slow signing speeds, pausing and holding a sign are some examples. You might sign fast, then slow, and then fast again to possibly show emotion.

Repetition – Repeating a sign, a rhythm, or classifier throughout the poem.

An example would be signing things in threes and beginning each repeated sign from right to middle to left. MY CLASS, CLASS, CLASS, I FAIL, FAIL, FAIL, TEACHER I MEET, MEET, MEET, ASK WHAT'S UP? WHAT'S UP? WHAT'S UP?

Signing space – Using the signing space; setting up various shapes or patterns in the space.

An example would be signing sections in an arc pattern, a circular pattern, or some linear pattern. The size of the sign can also be seen as a poetic device where you may sign something larger or smaller simply to emphasize an emotion or concept.

For more about ASL poetry, check out the videos and research by Ella Mae Lentz and Clayton Valli.

BASIC SONG TYPES

Another important concept to connect to acting and doing justice to the song is to consider the types of songs you are doing. We will discuss topics such as genre later. For now, let's look at the three basic song types.

There are three basic types:

The Multiple people – A song where two or more people interact in the song verbally or, in some instances, non-verbally, but they interact nonetheless; they are characters in the story.

Cyndi Lauper's "Girls Just Wanna Have Fun": Cyndi speaks, her mom speaks, and her dad speaks.

Gloria Gaynor's "I Will Survive": Even though the Ex who returns does not speak, she is talking to him—not to the audience.

The One Person "I" – A song where the person tells something that happened to them personally; they are a character in the story. This type of song also uses "I" statements, even though we, at times, may not be sure who the "I" person is.

Sweet Honey in the Rock's "Ain't Gonna Let Nobody Turn Me Round" is some unknown person telling that they will not accept racism any more, but will fight it.

In "Journey to the Past" from the animated film "Anastasia," the young girl remembers her life and talks about her love and family.

The Other people "He, She, They and You" – Recounts the events in a detached manner, simply telling what happened to someone else by talking about him, her, or them. This focus comes from someone, a narrator, who is not necessarily a character in the story but is someone talking about someone else in the story.

Peter Gabriel's "Biko": The narrator/reporter tells what happened to Steven Biko in South Africa in a documentary-like manner.

The Broadway musical *Rent* features the song "Seasons of Love", where someone talking about how to measure love.

What kind of song is it that you are going to do? This is important to know because it affects how you will set it up and present it. You have to be clear who is singing the song, who the song is being signed to, and who are you in relation to it (narrator, reporter, character in the story.) One other important thing to consider in answering this is: is the song gender specific? "Girls Just Wanna Have Fun" is a gender specific song.

If you are a male, can you perform that song? If you do, how do you choose to present it, when the pronouns in the song refer to you—the character—as a female?

So when you are figuring out the type of song, things like gender specificity arise for you to consider. So does character specificity, which is when the song is connected to a very specific setting and character. Girls Just Wanna Have Fun can be any girls, young, old, black, white, etc.

However, Madonna's version of "Don't cry For Me Argentina", in the musical *Evita*, is only Eva Peron singing to the people of Argentina. It is a very setting-oriented song. Being aware of that, as well, will affect the presentation and choice of a song to perform. Now, as I promised, let's talk about genre.

GENRE

The music industry has several genres that they use to classify music types or styles such as: R&B, Gospel, Rap, Alternative, Rock, Easy Listening, and Show tunes. One song can be performed or sung in several different genres. You as the ASL performer should carefully and consciously select genre, style, artist, and format to highlight your particular strengths and style. You do not want to select something that will showcase your weaknesses.

Cyndi Lauper's "Time After Time" is an example of a song that has crossed several genres as sung by various artists. Each artist has his or her own special feel or expression for the song and each is unique. The Cassandra Wilson version is slow and mellow while the Blaq version is a very upbeat, hip-hop style. You, the performer, as I said, must select the version that will highlight your skills and abilities.

Just as many people prefer to listen to a select style of music, you may choose to perform a select style of music. Know your strengths and weaknesses as well as your preferences. But be aware that by stretching and trying other styles, you will also grow and improve your skills. Growing beyond your comfort zone and thinking outside of the box are both very effective skills to develop.

I also want to take a moment to single out spiritual music. There are many religious interpreters desiring more information about interpreting Christian music, so I am including a small section for them.

Note: All of the other principles, techniques, and exercises throughout this book apply to Christian music just as it would for R&B or Rock.

Some Christian songs that are very repetitious, some are very slow, very fast, are gender or character specific, etc. However, one of the most important things to keep in mind is the "why" of Christian music.

I mentioned before that all music is basically a mini-story and a mini-story has a reason for being told how it is told; there is a moral to the story. There is a reason the artist is performing this song. Often times it is for entertainment, but sometimes it is for education or inspiration. That is the "why" of the song. When considering Christian / spiritual music you must also consider the spiritual beliefs that are attached to the song. For this reason, interpreters are encouraged to interpret in settings that are within their own faith. For example, a Jewish interpreter would be best suited to interpret in a synagogue or other function where sacred Hebrew music is being done versus in a Catholic service. A Christian interpreting at a Buddhist conference may create a disharmony within the interpreter and cause the interpreting product to suffer.

If you are interested in interpreting Christian music then I strongly encourage you to do the following:

Read Scripture – Many Christian songs are taken directly from a Bible verse or reference a Bible verse. If you have no idea about the context of the verse, the people being spoken about, or the language used ("Hosanna," for example), then how can you put the song on your hands? The more familiar you are with the first source text (the Bible), the more familiar you will be with the second source text (the song lyrics) and the more effective you will be as the interpreter of the song.

Go beyond words – As I mentioned earlier in the text, do not do what the novice ASL user tends to do by seeking a sign-for-word match. There WILL be times when you encounter a word in the song that has no sign. If you are seeking a sign-for-word match, what are you left to do? It is much more effective to do as I am instructing you in this text - focus on the concept. Suppose you encounter the words *Golgotha*, *Trinity*, or *Temple*. What do you do if you do not know the sign for them? If you know the concept of the word and how it is being used then you do not need a sign for the word.

Golgotha – What does it mean?
It is the Hebrew equivalent for the English name Calvary, which was the location of Jesus' crucifixion. I have seen several different interpretations for this word. You would have to select what works best

for you. The concept is the place where Jesus was crucified. Here are a few examples of what I have seen in my travels:

PLACE THERE HAPPEN JESUS CRUCIFY-FINISH
HILL (MOUNTAIN) CROSS
SKULL (BONE) AREA
PLACE CROSS CROSS CROSS

Trinity – What does it mean?

It refers to the God-head of God the Father, God the Son, and God the Holy Spirit; the three in one. Generally, there is one sign that I see used for this word or concept and that sign would be fairly easy for you to find if you look in Elaine Costello's "Religious Signing" book or online at aslpro.com. However, let's say you cannot find the word. What would you sign? Here are a few examples of what I have seen in my travels:

GOD, JESUS, HOLY SPIRIT TOGETHER

3-as-1 or 3-in-1 signed in a manner that is similar to the sign for *both*. This, however, uses a 3 handshape behind open palm, then becomes a 1 handshape as it moves down and in front of the other hand.

GOD WHO? FATHER, SON, HOLY SPIRIT, THREE-THEM GOD

T-R-I-N-I-T-Y (spelled) MEANS WHAT? GOD CL:3 FATHER, SON, HOLY SPIRIT

Temple – What does it mean?

The meaning depends on how it is being used. Are we talking about an actual building, the body as a temple, or the symbolic use—such as when Jesus referenced the temple being destroyed and rebuilt in three days to represent his death and resurrection? Let's go with the place of worship, a building - like a church -- where you worship and praise God. The sign for "temple" is typically signed like "church"—a "C" is placed on the back of a closed fist—however, the "T" handshape is used for the word "temple." But again suppose you do not have a sign for the word or know a specific sign, what are other options? Here are a few examples of what I have seen in my travels:

KNOW CHURCH? T-E-M-P-L-E SAME

CHURCH, T-E-M-P-L-E SAME, BUILDING YOU GO WORSHIP

BUILDING PEOPLE GO-THERE FOR-FOR? WORSHIP, PRAY

So it is critically important for you to have a grasp of the language, terms, and meanings in Christian music and service. If you are interpreting in a religious setting, the deaf person is receiving the message by what YOU are conveying. If you are giving misinformation, then you are skewing the message.

The more you research, learn, and work on your critical thinking skills — as well as ASL skills – and the more you utilize your team, the better your overall product will be. Speaking of teams, I know that there are many pastors and ministers of music who are not cooperative with you, the interpreter; however, if you intend to continue to interpret in that church then you must find a way to get them to be cooperative team players or find a new team in either that church or in another.

TEXT ANALYSIS

As you look over the lyrics, the English words of the song you intend to perform, you will face a variety of textual concerns and as you face these concerns you have to keep in mind the following:

What is the overall meaning of the song?
What are the parts of the song that demonstrate that meaning?
What are the concepts that are presented that support that meaning?

For example – is the song a love song? How do you know? What in the song tells you it is a love song? Who is in love? What tells you who is in love? What kind of love: Love of mother for child, love of person for God, love of man for wife?

Similar to a script for a play or movie, all that you need to know usually can be found in the lines, if you read carefully enough and find the concepts. There will, however, be times you have to use your creative license for artistic freedom.

As I said before, part of your text (lyric) analysis will present certain challenges and many of those challenges will be due to the following, which we will look at more in depth in the next section:

Nonsense words –

Nonsense words are those words that have no real meaning, they are words made up for the song. What do you do with Nonsense words?

Examples: "Nonsense words"
Willy Wonka and the Chocolate Factory
Oompa Loompa songs

Wicked
"No Good Deed"

Mary Poppins
"Supercalifragilisticexpialidocious"

Poetry or poetic lyrics –

Poetry or poetic lyrics are those lines that have elements of poetry such as simile and metaphor. How do you make those comparisons and how do you make the "flowery" language that was meant for the ear into a visual language meant for the eye?

Examples: "Poetry" "Poetic language / lyrics"

Sarah McLaughlin
"Answer"

Eminem
"Lose Yourself"

Kimberly Locke
"8th World Wonder"

Bonnie Tyler
"Total Eclipse of the Heart"

Vanessa Carlton
"A Thousand Miles"

Rhyme –

Rhymes are those lines that sound the same. While most songs have some form of rhyme, there are some that use it in a more unique specific manner that highlights the rhyme. Words that rhyme for the poetry, flow, and sound of the song present an interesting challenge. How do you visually represent an auditory device such as rhyme?

Examples: "Rhyme"

Des'ree
"Life"

Simon and Garfunkel
"50 Ways to Leave Your Lover"

Chuck Berry
"Johnny B. Goode"

Repetition –

Repetition is when you have verses or choral lines that are repeated several times throughout the song. This also presents an interesting challenge for the ASL artist. How do you avoid boredom, yet still represent the song's repetition?

Examples: "Repetition"

Fred Hammond
"Blessings and Honor"

Tonex
"God Has Not 4got"

Harry Belafonte
"Amen"

Strong vocabulary –
Strong vocabulary is used in some songs. Strong vocabulary means it is a song that includes words that have no sign, are in a foreign language, or has a meaning you may not be familiar with due to its use.

Vocabulary – based wording like rampart presents various dilemmas. How do you visually show certain English words that may have no sign? Since the general rule regarding fingerspelling in a song is to avoid it at all costs, what do you do?

Examples: "Strong Vocabulary"

Little Mermaid
"Under The Sea"

"Star Spangled Banner"

"Battle Hymn of the Republic"

Rent
"La Vie Boheme"

Sandi Patti
"Via Dolorosa"

Implicit or Implied –
Implicit or implied language can be tricky in several ways depending on what is being implied. The lyrics may imply something about love or suicide or could even imply something sexual. Some songs are very direct and you know exactly what is being sung about, while other songs have hidden or implied meaning. When you are faced with a song lyric that is not explicitly presented, how do you choose if and when or how to handle such implicit or implied meaning? What do you do with sexually implicit language?

Examples: "Implicit or Implied"

Chicago
"Mama"

Chuck Berry
"My Ding A Ling"

La Cage Aux Folles
"I Am What I Am"
"We Are What We Are"

Christine Aguilera
"Candyman"

Unknown meaning or context –
Unknown context or meaning is when you encounter some songs that you simply have no idea what the song is about. There are some rare songs that you, the listener / performer, have no idea what the original meaning of the song is. Some songs simply take more research and careful investigation; however, there are some songs that still defy explanation. How do you visually perform something when you have unknown context or meaning?

Examples: "Unknown context or meaning"

Cat Stevens
"Moonshadow"
"Peace Train"

Barbara Streisand
"Send in the Clowns"

Eurythmics
"Sweet Dreams (Are Made of This)"

NONSENSE WORDS

When faced with nonsense words such as those given in the examples of Oompa Loompa songs from *Willy Wonka and the Chocolate Factory* or "Do-Re-Mi" from *Sound of Music* or "No Good Deed" from *Wicked* (see lyrics below), you, the performer, must create a way to show the concept for that nonsense word. "Think about why the word is being used" / "Think about what the word represents." Many times this can be done by creating a series of gestures that tie the nonsense word's concept into the overall theme of the song. Do not simply select any arbitrary gesture, think of the ASL poetic features and try to incorporate a meaningful gestural representation of the word. Remember that you are performing a song and each movement should "add" to the overall effect, success, and visual artistry of the song, not detract from it.

Consider all your possibilities as you try similar handshapes or movement patterns, gestures, dance movements, and signs.

Willy Wonka and the Chocolate Factory
"Oompa Loompa songs"

Oompa loompa doompety doo
I've got a perfect puzzle for you
Oompa loompa doompety dee
If you are wise you'll listen to me

Whitney Houston
"Exhale"
Shoop, Shoop, Shoop
Shoo Be Doop Shoop Shoop (yeah)
Shoo Be Doop Shoop Shoop
(All you got to say is shoo be doop)

Sometimes you'll laugh sometimes you'll cry
Life never tells us
The when's or why's

Wicked
"No Good Deed"

ELPHABA
(spoken) Fiyero!
(sung) Eleka nahmen nahmen Ah tum ah tum eleka nahmen
Eleka nahmen nahmen Ah tum ah tum eleka nahmen

Let his flesh not be torn let his blood leave no stain
Though they beat him let him feel no pain

Sound of Music
"Do-Re-Mi"

[Maria:]
Do-re-mi-fa-so-la-ti
[spoken]
Let's see if I can make it easy
Doe, a deer, a female deer
Ray, a drop of golden sun

And while I am thinking of Julie Andrews, let's take a quick look at "Supercalifragilisticexpialidocious" from *Mary Poppins*.

Mary Poppins
"Supercalifragilisticexpialidocious"

Mary Poppins:
Um diddle diddle diddle um diddle ay
Um diddle diddle diddle um diddle ay

It's...
Supercalifragilisticexpialidocious!

Other popular songs with nonsense words that you may want to look up and experiment how to gloss and sign:

Little Richard's "Tutti Frutti"
"A-wop-bop-a-loo-bop A-wop bam boom"

The Beatles's "Ob la di, ob la da"
"Ob la di, ob la da Life goes on."

Labelle's "Lady Marmalade"
"Gitchy gitchy ya ya tata."

The Crystals' "Da Doo Ron Ron"
"Da doo ron ron ron, da doo ron ron ron I saw him standing at a rock 'n' show."

Nelly's "Country Grammar"
"Shimmy shimmy Cocoa what?"

One thing I previously mentioned briefly (and will go into more detail later) is a vocal feature that many songs have, which falls under nonsense words — the use of vocalizations that have no meaning.

Examples of this include: humming, oohhs and aahhhs, mmms, as well as scatting, or other vocalized sounds in the song.

Many songs that I have mentioned, as well as many that you will encounter, include this particular feature. Look out for them and be aware of their presence – we will talk more about this soon.

Poetic Language

Signing poetry is one of those things that I have found many people have a very difficult time dealing with, mostly because hearing people are often obsessed with the English words of the poetry versus the concept. Once you have the concept of the poetics, you can effectively sign the song without fear of being unduly free.

It is possible to make the same poetic comparisons in ASL that you would in English; however, ASL makes those comparisons visually.

Kimberly Locke's "8th World Wonder" makes the comparison of the boyfriend to the Seven Wonders of the World and he is what she calls the eighth world wonder. Obviously, this guy must be great because she is comparing him to such things as the Grand Canyon, Eiffel Tower, etc. But the challenge you have is how to show such comparisons without listing those other seven wonders.

Bonnie Tyler's "Total Eclipse of the Heart" talks about the total eclipse of the heart, if you break it down and analyze the meaning you will find the concept. What is an eclipse? What is a partial versus total eclipse? What would it mean for the heart to be eclipsed? Those are some of the types of questions you ask as you go through the analysis of the lyrics.

Sarah McLaughlin
"Answer"

Cast me gently into morning for the night has been unkind
Take me to a place so holy that I can wash this from my mind
The memory of choosing not to fight

Eminem
"Lose Yourself"

His palms are sweaty, knees weak, arms are heavy
There's vomit on his sweater already, mom's spaghetti
He's nervous, but on the surface he looks calm and ready
To drop bombs, but he keeps on forgettin what he wrote down

Kimberly Locke
"8th World Wonder"

Seven days and seven nights of thunder,
The waters rising and I'm slipping under.
I think I fell in love with the 8th world wonder.

Bonnie Tyler
"Total Eclipse of the Heart"

Your love is like a shadow on me all of the time
I don't know what to do and I'm always in the dark
We're living in a powder keg and giving off sparks
I really need you tonight

Vanessa Carlton
"A Thousand Miles"

If I could fall into the sky,
Do you think time would pass me by?
'Cause you know I'd walk a thousand miles
If I could just see you... Tonight.

RHYME

Many songs incorporate rhyme. Some songs rely more on the rhyming devise than others. Regardless of why the song relies on the rhyming device or the degree to which the song uses it, you have to find a way to make that auditory devise work in a visual performance. Again, the most important thing to remember is let go of the English words! ASL is based on concepts, not words. Once you can let go of the obsession with the English words and the rhyme, you can better utilize the visual possibilities that are inherent in the *conceptual* presentation of the lyrics. ASL poetic devices become a possible tool for you to use.

Des'ree
"Life"

Life oh life I'm afraid of the dark, 'Specially when I'm in a park
And there's no-one else around, Ooh, I get the shivers
I don't want to see a ghost, It's a sight that I fear most

Simon and Garfunkel
"50 Ways to Leave Your Lover"

Chorus:
Just slip out the back, Jack
Make a new plan, Stan
Don't need to be coy, Roy
Just listen to me

Chuck Berry
"Johnny B. Goode"

Deep down Louisiana close to New Orleans
Way back up in the woods among the evergreens
There stood a log cabin made of earth and wood
Where lived a country boy named Johnny B. Goode

Little Mermaid
"Under The Sea"

Even the sturgeon and the ray, they get the urge 'n start to play.
We've got the spirit. You've got to hear it. Under the sea.
The newt play the flute, the carp play the harp.
The plaice play the base and they soundin' sharp.

Rent
"La Vie Boheme"

MARK
To loving tension, no pension to more than one dimension,
To starving for attention, hating convention, hating pretension,
Not to mention of course, hating dear old mom and dad

REPETITION

There are some songs that have a key chorus or main line that is repeated several times. To many people that seems like a blessing. If you only have to do one sentence 10 times, that song has to be easy . . . right? Well, yes and no. Having a song that repeats is difficult if you want the song to be visually pleasing. It is very easy to get stuck in a rut and have the song be boring. My suggestion is to think of several ways you can convey the concept of the song and alter the signs every so often to keep it visually interesting while remaining true to the song by keeping the concept.

Fred Hammond
"Blessings and Honor"

Blessing and honor oh God Glory and power of God
Dominion forever, forever

Thy throne oh God will last forever, will last forever, forever

Tonex
"God Has Not 4got"

God has not 4got (repeat 4 times)
If He said that He would do it
It will come to pass
God has not 4got (repeat 2 times)

Harry Belafonte
"Amen"

Amen (repeat 10 times)
See the little baby, Amen
Wrapped in a manger Amen
On Christmas morning, Amen, Amen, Amen

STRONG VOCABULARY

Some songs have very strong, specific vocabulary and many of us have the tendency to obsess over the specific English word. If you dwell on the word, you will remain stuck. You have no recourse but to rely on your grasp of the concept. As I said before, make use of the various tools you have available, one of which is your dictionary. Once you have a meaning for the word, you can focus on the concept.

The "Star Spangled Banner" uses words such as rampart, twilight, spangled, and gleaming. While the words may not be all that difficult to comprehend, it is easy for some to obsess the specific words trying to find a sign for each word. Your task is to focus on the concept, NOT the word. In the "Under the Sea" example below, you have specific fish names to address: Sturgeon, Ray, Carp, etc.

Little Mermaid
"Under The Sea"

The fluke is the duke of soul. The ray he can play.
The lings on the strings. The trout rockin' out.
The blackfish she sings. The smelt and the sprat they know where it's at. An' oh that blowfish blow.

THE STAR-SPANGLED BANNER / The National Anthem
Oh, say, can you see, by the dawn's early light,
What so proudly we hailed at the twilight's last gleaming?
Whose broad stripes and bright stars, thro' the perilous fight'
O'er the ramparts we watched, were so gallantly streaming.
And the rockets red glare, the bombs bursting in air,
Gave proof through the night that our flag was still there.
Oh, say, does that star-spangled banner yet wave

O'er the land of the free and the home of the brave?

{**This next part is rarely sung but is still a good exercise to translate especially for those rare times when it is sung.}

On the shore dimly seen, thro' the mists of the deep,
Where the foe's haughty host in dread silence reposes,
What is that which the breeze, o'er the towering steep,
As it fitfully blows, half conceals, half discloses?
Now it catches the gleam of the morning's first beam,
In full glory reflected, now shines on the stream;
'Tis the star-spangled banner: oh, long may it wave
O'er the land of the free and the home of the brave.

And where is that band who so vauntingly swore
That the havoc of war and the battle's confusion
A home and a country should leave us no more?
Their blood has wash'd out their foul footstep's pollution.
No refuge could save the hireling and slave
From the terror of flight or the gloom of the grave,
And the star-spangled banner in triumph doth wave
O'er the land of the free and the home of the brave.

Oh, thus be it ever when free men shall stand,
Between their loved homes and the war's desolation;
Blest with vict'ry and peace, may the heav'n-rescued land
Praise the Power that has made and preserved us as a nation.
Then conquer we must, when our cause is just,
And this be our motto: "In God is our trust";
And the star-spangled banner in triumph shall wave
O'er the land of the free and the home of the brave.

BATTLE HYMN OF THE REPUBLIC
Mine eyes have seen the glory of the coming of the Lord;
He is trampling out the vintage where the grapes of wrath are stored;
He hath loosed the fateful lightning of His terrible swift sword;

His truth is marching on.
Glory! Glory! Hallelujah! Glory! Glory! Hallelujah!
Glory! Glory! Hallelujah! His truth is marching on.
I have seen Him in the watch fires of a hundred circling camps
They have builded Him an altar in the evening dews and damps;
I can read His righteous sentence by the dim and flaring lamps;
His day is marching on.
Glory! Glory! Hallelujah! Glory! Glory! Hallelujah!
Glory! Glory! Hallelujah! His day is marching on.
I have read a fiery Gospel writ in burnished rows of steel;
"As ye deal with My contemners, so with you My grace shall deal";
Let the Hero, born of woman, crush the serpent with His heel,
Since God is marching on.
Glory! Glory! Hallelujah! Glory! Glory! Hallelujah!
Glory! Glory! Hallelujah! Since God is marching on.
He has sounded forth the trumpet that shall never call retreat;
He is sifting out the hearts of men before His judgment seat;
Oh, be swift, my soul, to answer Him! be jubilant, my feet;
Our God is marching on.
Glory! Glory! Hallelujah! Glory! Glory! Hallelujah!
Glory! Glory! Hallelujah! Our God is marching on.
In the beauty of the lilies Christ was born across the sea,
With a glory in His bosom that transfigures you and me:
As He died to make men holy, let us live to make men free;
[originally …let us die to make men free]
While God is marching on.
Glory! Glory! Hallelujah! Glory! Glory! Hallelujah!
Glory! Glory! Hallelujah! While God is marching on.
He is coming like the glory of the morning on the wave,
He is wisdom to the mighty, He is honor to the brave;

So the world shall be His footstool, and the soul of wrong His slave,
Our God is marching on.
Glory! Glory! Hallelujah! Glory! Glory! Hallelujah!
Glory! Glory! Hallelujah! Our God is marching on.

Rent
"La Vie Boheme"

MIMI & ANGEL
To hand-crafted beers made in local breweries
To yoga, to yogurt, to rice and beans and cheese
To leather, to dildos, to curry Vindaloo
To Huevos Rancheros, and Maya Angelou

IMPLICIT OR IMPLIED

This is one of my favorite areas simply because of the challenge it offers. Many songs have a word or phrase that has several possible meanings and connotations. For example, the word modern means "belonging to recent times," but the word's connotations can include such notions as "new, up to date, and experimental."

Euphemism **is** the substitution of an agreeable or inoffensive expression for one that may offend or suggest something unpleasant. One example is the numerous euphemisms within the English language related to death and dying. The practice of using euphemisms for death is likely to have originated with the "magical belief that to speak the word 'death' was to invite death; where to 'draw death's attention' is the ultimate bad fortune"—a common theory holds that death is a taboo subject in most English-speaking cultures for precisely this reason. It may be said that one is not dying, but fading quickly because the end is near. People who have died are referred to as "having passed away" or "passed" or "departed." Deceased is a euphemism for "dead" and sometimes the deceased is said to have gone to a better place, but this is used primarily among the religious with a concept of Heaven.

Sexual innuendo is one prime example where the word could have a double meaning. Examples: Pussy (vagina, cat, a weak man, or "wimp"), Dick (penis, short for Richard, or private detective.)

The suggested meaning may be implicit in the words used or the additional meaning may be implied in how it is sung.

Chicago
Queen Latifah
"When You're Good to Mama"

[MATRON]
They say that life is tit for tat and that's the way I live
So, I deserve a lot of tat for what I've got to give

If you want my gravy Pepper my Ragu
Spice it up for Mama she'll get hot for you

Chuck Berry
"My Ding-a-Ling"

When I was a little biddy boy my grandma bought me a cute little toy
Two silver bells on a string she told me it was my ding-a-ling-a-ling

My Ding-A-Ling My Ding-A-Ling won't you play with My Ding-A-Ling

Christina Aguielera
"Candyman"

He's a one stop shop, make my cherry pop
He's a sweet-talkin', sugar coated candy man
Well by now I'm getting all bothered and hot

La Cage Aux Folles
"I Am What I Am"

I am what I am I am my own special creation.
So come take a look, give me the hook or the ovation.
It's my world that I want to take a little pride in,
My world, and it's not a place I have to hide in.

La Cage Aux Folles
"We Are What We Are"

Les Cagelles:
We are what we are and what we are is an illusion.
We love how it feels putting on heels causing confusion.
We face life though it's sometimes sweet and sometimes bitter;
Face life, with a little guts and lots of glitter.

UNKNOWN MEANING OR CONCEPT

What do you do when you are not sure what the song is about or you cannot quite find the moral of the story so to speak? There are many songs out there that are like abstract art; you look at the painting again and again and again and you still have no idea what the painting is of or what the artist is trying to say. In the same way, songs are like abstract art in that you aren't always sure what the song is about or what the artist is trying to say. You, the performer, have a few options. You can present it in a manner that is also vague and hard to comprehend or you can present what you perceive the song to be about. Figure out what the song means to you and present that to the audience.

Vanessa Carlton
"1,000 Miles"

If I could fall into the sky,
Do you think time would pass me by?
'Cause you know I'd walk a thousand miles
If I could just see you... Tonight.

Cat Stevens
"Moonshadow"

I'm being followed by a moon shadow
Moon shadow-moon shadow
Leaping and hopping on a moon shadow
Moon shadow-moon shadow

Cat Stevens
"Peace Train"

Peace train sounding louder
Ride on the peace train
Hoo-ah-eeh-ah-hoo-ah
Come on the peace train

Barbara Streisand
"Send In the Clowns"

Don't you love farce?
My fault, I fear.
I thought that you'd want what I want - Sorry, my dear.
But where are the clowns?

Sweet Dreams (Are Made of These)
Annie Lennox

Sweet dreams are made of this, who am I to disagree?
I travel the world and the seven seas
Everybody's looking for something.

CHRISTIAN MUSIC

It has been my experience that many interpreters in religious settings desire more guidance, assistance, and suggestions on how to fully render music during worship services. Since 1992, I have been observing, learning, putting into practice and gathering the information contained within this text. In order to further address some of what I mentioned earlier with Christian music, let's look at some examples of Christian songs with possible glossing samples as well.

Yolanda Adams
"Victory"

All my battle's He'll fight
MY FRUSTRATION STRUGGLE HE-F SEIZE (adopt)

I got got the victory
I WIN, HAVE SUCCESS

I got the sweet, sweet victory in Jesus
HAVE WONDERFUL WIN SUCCESS WHY? CONNECT JESUS

Crystal Lewis
"Joyful Joyful"

Melt the clouds of sin and sadness. Drive the dark of doubt away
HAPPEN WE SAD, SIN YOU-F PUSH-ASIDE (left)
HAPPEN WE DOUBT YOU-F THROW-AWAY (right)

Giver of immortal gladness. Fill us with the light of day
YOU-F GIVE-US HAPPY FOREVER YOU-F GIVE-US
BEAUTIFUL INSPIRE BRIGHT DAY

Josh Groban
"Oh Holy Night"

O Holy night, the stars are brightly shining.
HOLY NIGHT THERE STARS CL:55 SHINE BRIGHT

It is the night of our dear Saviour's birth.
NIGHT NOW HAPPEN WHAT? OUR CHERISH (2 hands)
SAVIOR HE-F BORN FINISH

Long lay the world in sin and error pining,
WORLD, PEOPLE LONG TIME SINCE, SIN WRONG,
HEART-BREAK SUFFER, STRESS

Whitney Houston
"Joy to the World"

Joy to the world the Lord is come
LET WORLD YOU-F (double hands) NOW HAPPY. WHY?
LORD HE-F BORN-FINISH

Let Earth receive her king
LET EARTH YOU-F (left hand) ACCEPT (right) WHO? (left)
YOUR (left) KING (right) HIM-F

Let every heart prepare him room
NOW ALL PEOPLE YOUR HEART, LET HIM-F CONNECT,
RELATIONSHIP

Kirk Franklin
"Hosanna"

So the angels bow down at the thought of You
ANGEL HUMBLE CL:fist (bow) HAPPEN FACE-TO-FACE
(God) BOW

The darkness brings way to the light for You
DARK FADE WHY? YOU-F LIGHT

The price that you paid gives us life brand new
YOUR SACRIFICE CRUCIFY GIVE-US-F WHAT? NEW
LIFE

Hosanna forever we worship You
PRAISE FOREVER WE-F WORSHIP JESUS YOU-F

TRANSLATION

The translation process is probably the one thing that most people I have met and taught have found most daunting. People seem to honestly dislike the translation and glossing process. Well, I can completely understand their trepidation. I am not a linguist so my translation and glossing process is not what someone with a PhD in linguistics would do; however, I know that I will not improve and learn if I do not complete the task to the best of my ability. The glosses I would do today are not the glosses of five years ago. Improvement is inevitable if you do the work. Each of us as interpreters, students, teachers, or performers must do what is most comfortable for us where we are in the journey to proficiency.

As I just said, the way I gloss now is not the same as five years ago and in five years it will again be different, if I continue to work at and develop the skill. That is one important thing to remember: this is a journey, not a destination. It is precisely that reason that I have not *given* you the answers to many of the examples listed. It has been my experience that giving people the answers allows their ego to keep them in their comfort zone rather than stepping out into unchartered territory. By being encouraged to analyze and contemplate, you exercise those ASL muscles. There is never a time when you learn all of ASL. It is like English, do you know every English word, the rules, how every word is spelled or, used, and their meaning? For most of us, the answer is no. English is a journey as well. As a language, it will change and evolve over time. Think about it: in the 80s there was no such word as email, laptop or plasma TV; there was no Video Relay or Video Phone. These words were introduced to the lexicon and are now part of our language. Start where you are with your current skill and do the best you can and, as time progresses, you will learn to do more efficient and effective translations and glosses.

The most important skill to develop in your translation process is comprehension of the languages you are using - in this case ASL and English. You must have an understanding of both in order to do an effective and accurate translation.

I have noticed many times people will find an English word, "obsess" over it, and search for a sign-to-word match. Many beginning ASL students believe that there is a sign for every English word. They do not realize that it is not the word you are matching, but the concept.

For example, the word "may" has several ways to be signed based upon the concept. It is not the word being signed, but the concept of the word as it is used in a sentence.

In May, I may ask May if I may go to Florida.

In May (the month) I may (maybe, might, possibly will) ask May (person's name), if I may (am permitted to, can) go to Florida.

So you have a single English word that will have multiple concepts / meanings.

You have English idioms and slang that also have various conceptual meanings.

What sign would you use to match the concept of the following words?

In the *aftermath* of Katrina, the city was left in *ruins*.

Due to his behavior, the student was *detained* until his parents could *pick him up*.

My brother has the worst *pick up* lines ever!

My granddad's old *pickup* is in our garage.

It's late. I have to *run*. See you tomorrow.

My car broke down and no matter what they do, it won't *run*.

Is your dad really going to *run* for governor?

Does your nose *run* when your allergies flare up?

She stopped wearing stockings because she always gets a *run* in them.

Can I stay at your *pad*? My *old lady kicked* me out.

When did old man Wilkins *kick the bucket*?

He *passed* six years after his wife *bought the farm*.

[Are we talking about someone taking a class or someone dying? And did she literally buy a farm or did she also die?]

Tim and his older brother are *tight*.

You need to buy a new pair of pants. Those are too *tight*.

Karen's new tattoo is *tight*.

If the DVD won't play, we can go to a *play*.

Don't *play* with matches.

Don't *play* with me; I am not in the mood.

A friend of ours is *playing* in a band tonight.

When his wife is out of town he *plays the field*.

If you *play your hand right*, you may get that promotion

I hope you sort of get the idea after having read the preceding sentences. The English must be grasped in order to understand the initial intent and meaning, but once you understand that, you must then understand ASL well enough to select the most appropriate and effective way to sign and communicate that intent and meaning. You cannot be literal in your translation lest you convey the wrong meaning.

She married him after six months of him hitting on her.

Hitting on? Does it mean flirting with or abuse? In that sentence it could be taken as either depending on the context and intent of the speaker. If you signed it literally—"hitting on" to mean abuse, when in reality the intent is to flirt - isn't the meaning changed, and in that change are you not giving an incorrect message?

You have to be sure that you understand before you put it on your hands. As you begin to understand and conceptualize the meaning, you must then consider how to sign it. Use your ASL grammatical tools and sentence structure to compose the translation. "The Rule of 3" is one important concept that I learned and now use when translating, glossing, and signing, or performing and I encourage you to master it as well.

The Rule of "3"

It's interesting that The Rule of 3 is actually a concept that I learned from practicing martial arts. A skilled warrior has a myriad of ways to defend against a single punch. The minute you think there is only one way, you will be hit. The Rule of 3 again appeared in my life as an acting term and concept that I learned while a graduate student at Virginia Commonwealth University in the MFA, Theatre Pedagogy program. I have since taken that martial art / acting tool and have applied it to various areas of my creative life: my drawing, choreographing, and signing.

The rule simply means that there are at least three ways to do something.

For the purposes of this text, you need to know that there are at least 3 ways for you to sign the concept.

The concept:
Someone is explaining that their mother asked them to go to the store tomorrow, on their way home, to get four items: milk, bread, eggs, and ice cream. This could be signed several ways.

Possible English statements:
Version 1: My mother asked me if I would pick up a few things on my way home tomorrow. She wants me to get bread, milk, eggs, and ice cream.

Version 2: I am going to pick up a few things from the store tomorrow on my way home because my mother asked me to.

Version 3: My mom asked me if I would get bread, milk, eggs and ice cream tomorrow on my way home.

That satisfies the rule of 3 but I am sure if you think about it, you could think of several more possible ways to say it in English to convey the same concept.

Having thus come up with three English versions, you would then translate into ASL and again you should have at least three possible varieties.

Tomorrow I what-do? Go store. I get bread, milk, eggs, ice cream because mom asked me.

My mother ask me what? Tomorrow go store, buy 4 things. Bread, milk, eggs, ice cream.

Tomorrow before I go home, I go store because mother want me to buy milk, ice cream, eggs, and bread.

Again, I could go on with several more possible ways to sign the concept. Work diligently at not becoming stuck, as many do, thinking that there is only one way to sign something. Even something as simple as "stop" can be expressed at least three ways depending on what you are attempting to convey in ASL.

When working on songs, it is not always easy to know what the lyricist means. That is one of those things about poetry. The words used do not always mean what they are saying. Symbolism, allusion, simile and metaphor often cloud our perceptions. However, I am here to tell you that you can still sign the song. Remember earlier I spoke to you about the tools you have access to? You have a myriad of possible research tools available to you. One of my personal favorite examples of a metaphor that I like to give my students is –

All the world's a stage,
And all the men and women merely players;
They have their exits and their entrances
(William Shakespeare, *As You Like It*, 2/7)

You have libraries where you can go look up things related to poetry and symbolism. You have people you can ask who may be versed in such things and you have the internet as a means of research. Often times the artist / lyricist or a fan has a website where they may explain the song's meaning. Make use of the tools at your disposal. Also remember that the way you sign a song today does not have to remain that way forever. As you progress / evolve in skill and understanding, your translations can and will also evolve. Relax and be a willing student who is open to change. The moment you become rigid and inflexible is when you stop learning and growing.

Beginning ASL students are also known to say things like, "I didn't learn to sign it that way."

For example one person may sign "how" and do it in a more formal manner—using both hands, yet the students later see someone do a more conversational version—which uses one hand. Because the conversational method was not what was learned, the student is quick to think it is wrong because it is different.

There are several ways that people sign just as there are several ways that people say things. Ma, mom, mommy, mother, mama all mean the same thing. Soda, soda pop, and pop are all words used for soft drinks. ASL does the same thing. There are accents, signing styles and regional differences, formal, conversational and other various reasons why signs may be slightly, or even drastically, different from person to person.

What is signed for SODA in one location is POISION in another location. Hence understanding the context and concept of what is being said is important, but so is being flexible and willing to adjust, to learn variations. One thing that classifies a language as a language is the fact that language changes over time . . . therefore should we not also be willing to change if we are using the language?

PUTTING THE SONG ON YOUR HANDS

Once you know what the song means and you have the concept in mind, you must figure out how to 'put it on your hands,' which means how to present that song in ASL. There are several things that I suggest you keep in mind as you are thinking about how to sign, and then perform, the song. Notice I said how to sign and THEN how to perform. Signing the song and performing the song are two different things. Signing a song does not involve many of the stages and principles that I am introducing in this text. So when you are performing, here are several things to keep in mind:

1. Articulation and clarity.

Whatever you are signing MUST be articulated in a manner that is understandable. Being aware of the ASL parameters also aids in articulation of your signs and greatly assists in clarity. Think of a public speaker who articulates and carefully enunciates his words, that is what knowledge of the parameters will do for your ASL – make it precise, accurate, and clear.

ASL parameters affect sign choice.
The five parameters of ASL: Location, Palm Orientation, Movement, Handshape, and Non-manual markers are very important in not only signing, but also vitally important in performing a song. One English word can have several possible sign choices based upon the concept of how the word is being used – for example – Run. Run has several possible ways to convey the concept depending on what is being spoken. If you are aware of the parameters, your sign choice as a performer becomes more artistic like a poet and writer who are very conscious of the words used or the painter who selects pigments very carefully. One example of how the parameters might affect your performance can be seen in the use of the ASL poetic device – Similar Handshape.

In the "The Lord's Prayer" you could sign as follows-
Our Father who art in heaven. . .
Using "B" handshapes in line with the poetry example I gave earlier, you could sign that as OUR GOD YOU IN HEAVEN

You cannot have that kind of creativity without keeping the parameters in mind.

2. Clear identification of referents and topic.
Another tool that will aid in being clear is identifying who or what you are referring to when it may not be explicit. Remember that I need to know what you are talking about before you tell me what happened to it.

"It blew up!"

What blew up? The house, the car, or his career blew up? I need to know in order to understand what you are saying.

Suppose you have the English sentence, "I need you to talk to him." In that sentence, you are referring to some male that needs to be spoken to. You cannot simply sign him and expect it to be clear. In order for clarity, you need to make reference to who "he" is. Likewise your boss asks, "Is it done?" If you do not already know what "it" is, how can you answer? You must know what is being referred to. Now an example of a song:

R. Kelly
"I Believe I Can Fly"

I used to think that I could not go on and life was nothing but an awful song
But now I know the meaning of true love I'm leaning on the everlasting arms
If I can see it, then I can do it if I just believe it, there's nothing to it

There are two referents that you have to make clear. What is the "it" you can see and do? And what is the "it" in which you just need to believe? The other question I have is what are the "everlasting arms" on which you are "learning"? Can you sign the exact phrase "everlasting arms" and have it understood or do you need to make that explicit and clear as well? I suggest you reference God versus referencing the "everlasting arms."

Michael Jackson's song "They Don't Care About Us" mentions several times that "They" don't care about "Us." Who are "They?" And who is the "Us" that he speaks about?

As you can see from this portion of the song, you would have to clarify the "They" and the "Us" rather early in order to be clear.

Michael Jackson
"They Don't Care About Us"

CHORUS: *(Children)
Skin head, dead head, everybody gone bad.
Situation, aggravation, everybody allegation.
In the suit, on the news, everybody dog food. Bang, bang, shock dead. Everybody's gone mad.

3. Clearly establish the timeline.
In order to follow the flow of the song, story, or events, you would be wise to set up the chronological timeline in which the events occurred. "My mother and brother rushed me to the hospital because I busted my head open while playing at home." What happened first?

Was I brought to the hospital first or did I bust my head first or was I playing first? Right, the playing happened first. Then head injury and finally the hospital. So for clarity, it makes more sense to say: "When I was playing at home, I busted my head open, so my mother and brother rushed me to the hospital." I was recently at a church and observed the interpreter sign this passage literally.

Genesis 6
1 And it came to pass, when men began to multiply on the face of the earth, and daughters were born unto them, 2 That the sons of God saw

the daughters of men that they were fair; and they took them wives of all which they chose. 3 And the LORD said, My spirit shall not always strive with man, for that he also is flesh: yet his days shall be an hundred and twenty years. 4 There were giants in the earth in those days; and also after that, when the sons of God came in unto the daughters of men, and they bare children to them, the same became mighty men which were of old, men of renown.

How do you set up the opening line, "and it came to pass..." What does that mean? It is a time reference and therefore must be clearly established. You cannot sign it literally "AND IT CAME TO PASS," and expect it to be clear. What is "it"? Who or what did "it" pass? See my point? So you must think about how you set up the timeline. The passage goes on to say, "...yet his days shall be an hundred and twenty years. . . There were giants in those days..."

In the song "Streets of Philadelphia" we see another example of time being used as the person in the story talks about things that occurred in the past and the present.

Bruce Springsteen

"Streets Of Philadelphia"
I was bruised and battered and I couldn't tell what I felt
I was unrecognizable to myself, I saw my reflection in a
Window I didn't know my own face Oh brother are you gonna
leave me wastin'away on the streets of Philadelphia

4. Grammatical, artistic, and cultural adjustments.
Be mindful of ASL sentence structure and know that there are times you will want to restructure the sentence in order to have comprehension as well as for dramatic effect.

Mario Lanza has a version of "The Lord's Prayer" which he sings very slowly. I have seen very few people perform it in a manner that was interesting and visually pleasing. I want to use one line from the song to demonstrate grammatical changes for emphasis.

"Hallowed be thy name."

Holding the last sign "NAME" is less interesting or emphatic than saying "YOUR NAME HOLY." Also, in order to fill some of the time that the singer holds a note, you can add more emphasis by signing "YOUR NAME WOW TRUE-BIZ HOLY"

Many times music and theatre use poetic language, metaphor, simile, or symbolism. Even in daily conversation, we incorporate poetic elements when we say things like, "He's in a better place" or "Don't sweat the small stuff." "Don't cut your nose to spite your face." "Time waits for no man." "What goes around comes around." "Kill two birds with one stone." To get to the meaning of the phrase, the concept is your first task. Once you have done that, then you can get creative.

In order to adequately portray these aspects, I strongly recommend developing your ASL poetry skills. I spoke in depth about this earlier, so I will not repeat that information here. I just wanted to reemphasize the importance of developing the skills.

In conversation and in song, there references made to 'hearing;' such references can be altered by making a cultural adjustment. For example: "You hear what I'm saying to you?" Actually means "DO YOU UNDERSTAND?" The phrase "Did you hear on the news. . .?", can be adjusted by signing NEWS, DID YOU SEE. . .? Or KNOW NEWS? HAVE STORY ABOUT. . .DID YOU SEE?

Christmas songs are filled with sound references. "Do you hear what I hear?" "I heard the bells on Christmas day." "Sleigh bells ring, are you listening?" How would you make the appropriate adjustments?

5. Repetition.
Often times—in music especially—there are lines, phrases, or words that are repeated. Earlier, I gave you several examples. I simply want to take the time now to remind you that you have creative license and are encouraged to step out of the box in order to increase interest and break-up the monotony that often occurs from seeing songs that have lots of repetition.

6. Setting up the song.
There are times during a musical prelude, interlude, postlude, or moment when the singer is humming (or performing one of the other vocalizations that I spoke of previously) that you could use as "set-up"

or "explanation" time. Remember one of my previous examples about "Lamb of God" as one of the names of Jesus? You have the possible option of explaining this name during the musical prelude. As you set the scene, you can also explain and clarify other things as well, including names, titles, locations, or placement of people.

7. Variety.

When dealing with music, theatre, poetry, etc., there are a vast number of possible things you can face – words in other languages, words spoken to fast or too slow, words in which you are not sure of the meaning or context, etc. My best advice to you is preparation. The more time you invest in studying the text you will work from, the better your final product will be. Do not be afraid of variety . . . remember that variety is the spice of life.

8. Tone of the song.

As you perform or interpret, you must remember to match the tone of the speaker or song. If it is humorous, you should portray the humor. If it is tender and sweet, you must also match the mood and feeling of the song. This is where signing style really comes into play.

SIGNING STYLE

As I mentioned, each person has a particular signing style just as each person has distinctive handwriting. Each is unique and different. Think of several fonts and how they are different, yet have the same basis.

Raymont

Raymont

Raymont

Raymont

Raymont

Raymont

Raymont

Raymont

Be aware of your own particular style so that when you perform you are mindful of – and in control of—the style. Be aware of the following:

Size – How big are your signs? Are you signing to be seen by the people in the last row of the theater? Is the size of your signs representative of the tone, pace, quality of the song? Are your performing signs the same size as the signs you use when conversing?

As a performer, you must sign larger than you would in regular conversation or most interpreting situations.

Clarity – Are you clear in your style? Are the concepts clearly presented and are the signs produced clearly?

Do not fumble, bumble, or jumble your signs together. Be clear in your sign production. When in doubt, ask someone for feedback. Also videotape yourself and be honest in your self-critique.

Speed – Does your speed reflect the pace and tone of the song? What does your speed show or say to the audience? How clear are you when you sign faster? Are you comfortable with slow or fast songs? It is also important to be aware of your skill in reference to speed. Some people cannot sign fast and be clear. One challenge that slower songs present (that many people do not really think about) are those long-held notes.) Are your signs also conveying the held note? For example, suppose the last word sung is "No" and is held long and sung slow… "Noooooooooooooooooooo"

How do you sign "No" in a manner that reflects the vocalist who may be holding the note or singing slow? Ahhh, now you see the challenge. There is also the option of not conveying the note at all since it is an auditory thing that represents the vocalist's skill. I would challenge you to play with your options.

Sometimes, depending on how you present the concept of the song, you have the option of altered word order, and you may be able to place a different sign on the end of the line that is more suitable and effective.

Register of character (singer) – How are you matching or representing the singer's vocal quality and presentation? For example, suppose Bette Midler is singing a line and imitating Grouch Marx. Is your visual presentation also showing such represented differences? How do you visually show such changes or differences in what the singer does with the voice? Can you show a bass versus tenor voice?

Be aware of the mood and attitude of the vocalist and match that mood and attitude in your style. Note that there are times (more for hearing people's aesthetic) when the register of a female singer would be most effectively done by a female ASL performer. Generally, unless there is gender specific language, gender matching is not a major factor in performing. I have several female vocalists' songs as part of my repertoire and the presentation is effective and enjoyable.

PUTTING THE SONG ON YOUR BODY

So now, you know how to begin putting the song on your hands and I applaud you. That is, however, not enough; you cannot stop there. Now, I charge you to go the next level. How do you put the song on your entire body? Before you can answer that, you may want to know why you should even consider putting it on your body. As a performer whose tool - and whose instrument – is your body (ASL incorporates more than just your hands), you want to have a full grasp and full use of the entire range of your body. ASL storytellers like Manny Hernandez and ASL poets like Ella Mae Lentz utilize their whole body in their art forms; it is more than just what they do with the hands. So for maximum effect, there are times when you will be incorporating more than signs into your presentation / performance. There are also times when there are no vocals to be signed.

What do you do when you have musical preludes, interludes or postludes with no text? In addition to musical moments, there are also moments where certain performers make vocalizations, as I mentioned earlier, that are not words; they use humming or "ohhs" and "ahhs" or they scat. At those moments, you are still required to put the song on your body. The following is a brief list of performers that I expose my students to because they offer challenges to the ASL performing artist who does not have command of his or her body in performing.

Bobby McFerrin
Al Jarreau
Josh Groban
Tuck and Patti
Sweet Honey in the Rock*

*Note: I want to make special mention of this particular group. Sweet Honey in the Rock has a member of their acappella performance group who interprets / performs all of their music in ASL. Shirley Childress Saxton is wonderfully skilled and a beautiful example of what one can and should do when faced with non-vocals and when challenged with full body musicality. (See the PBS documentary American Masters 'Raise Your Voice' when Sweet Honey was featured.)

Part of putting the song on your body that will also be discussed in the next section is showing the beat, the rhythm, of the song. That could be done *by simply* tapping your foot to the beat or moving your body to the beat or actually signing in a particular rhythm. All of that incorporates dance-like movements. Just as a hearing audience member is entertained by the auditory pleasure of the music itself, you must embody the music, make the music visual. Give access to the visual qualities of the music based upon your own personal interpretation of the music. Show the music visually by using your body. Just as five different painters could see the same rose and paint five totally different renditions of the rose, you must create your visual masterpiece using your entire being as your canvas, paints, and subject matter.

You are the movie screen, the actors, the characters, the soundtrack, and the musical score all in one body.

Dance / Movement

Though I spoke about this earlier in the book, I want to reiterate some of the key concepts for you now that you have a deeper grasp and more ample palette from which to paint. Incorporating a degree of dance and / or movement patterns can also be very beneficial to the ASL performer and interpreter. You will increase the movement vocabulary and range of what you are capable of doing when performing or interpreting. How a performer embodies dance / movement is unique and particular to the performer – you.

Some of my suggestions on how you can begin to do this are:
- Take a class
- Borrow or buy instructional dance videos
- Rent movies that have dance in them and observe
- Go to dance shows and observe
- Watch music videos and observe
- Observe movement in general

The more you see movement and dance, the more it will increase your movement vocabulary. As you become comfortable, begin to add more movement into your performance (at appropriate moments) that do not distract from the ASL, but support the ASL and increase the visual pleasure of the song overall.

Preparation to Perform

An often neglected—but vitally important—activity that both interpreters and performer fail to do is warm up. Both interpreters and ASL performers need to warm up before working, rehearsing, and performing, just as all professionals do before they begin the activity. Basketball players and all athletes warm up before they begin. All dancers warm up before beginning the choreography. Authors warm up by getting all their materials and their writing space in order. The painter preps his materials before touching the canvas. As a professional, you must warm up as well.

A basic warm up consists of:

Relaxation exercises that help warm up your muscles as well as release tension that can cause injuries. Here are a few simple exercises that may assist you.

Breathing

You would not think that people neglect to breathe but many of us do not breathe correctly for maximum health and well-being. We do not breathe in a manner that is relaxing, effective for awareness, or stimulating for creativity. If you take a deep breath, right now and hold it for a count of ten seconds….go ahead, do it. While doing it, notice what your body is doing. Did your chest and shoulders rise? Or did your abdomen rise? If your chest and shoulders rose, then you are cheating yourself of much needed oxygen. Filling only the upper portion of your lungs neglects the lower portion and does not give you full oxygen capacity. The more oxygen your brain and cells receive, the more alert, aware, and capable you are. Taking several deep abdominal breaths can do wonders for replenishing energy, calming nerves, and releasing fears and tension. Slowly inhale, hold for a few seconds, then slowly exhale and repeat several times.

Meditation
Earlier in the text, I gave you a centering exercise (which is the essence of a meditation) so I will not repeat that here. I will, however, remind you of the importance of having a calm, clear mind. If your mind is on auto-pilot or in default mode and you are thinking of a thousand and one things, how can you focus and be the most effective with the task of interpreting? Do you want the surgeon that is focused on the scalpel and monitors or the one thinking about his dinner appointment later that evening?

Breathe and be presently mindful of now.

Tension release
Many of us walk around all day carrying tension that we do not even realize we have and that tension creates chronic back and neck pains, swollen and painful joints, and more. One way of identifying tension so you can release it is by actively tensing the muscle and then releasing that tension. Clench your fist as tightly as you can comfortably clench, hold it for a few seconds and then release it. Feel the difference? If not, do it again, several times, so that you can easily feel what tension feels like. As you become more aware of the tension, do not clench quite so hard, but still clench and release. Do that several times as well and be aware of the subtle differences now. Then, clench again even less than before and continue this to develop greater awareness of the tension. Do the same thing with your arms, neck, teeth and jaw, chest, abdomen, legs, buttocks, feet and toes. Clench and tighten the muscles then release and repeat and be aware. The more you develop the awareness, the more able you will be to identify the subtle tension you may be holding as you approach the job or stage to perform or interpret. If you can identify it, you can release it.

Massaging, stretching body, arms, and hands (getting the blood circulating.)
When you can get a massage, it is great, but what I am going to talk to you about right now is what you can do for yourself by your self. Simply

rubbing your arms, legs, and hands will increase blood circulation and thus increase oxygen flow. Rubbing your hands together—like we do when it is cold—creates warmth because of the friction and increased blood flow. Why wait for the snow and cold to do the same thing and reap the same benefits? Warm muscles function better and longer than cold muscles.

Stretching of not only your body, but of your arms and hands, is also often neglected. I often do the alphabet before I interpret or perform because it stretches my fingers and wrist and gets them ready to work. If you want carpal tunnel or repetitive stress injuries, don't stretch and warm up. Also doing things like shoulder shrugs, head circles and raising your arms above your head can assist in providing a basic stretch. For more thorough stretching, see the resource list in the appendix. Again, the more you prep your body to work, the better it will work for you.

PERFORMING AND HOLISM

As a life long student of philosophy, spirituality, world religions, the New Thought Movement, and metaphysics, I have come across some rather amazing discoveries and would like to share a few with you as I bring this text to a close. The main reason I am sharing this with you is because of the benefit that you can bring to yourself and your audience through your signing.

In our everyday use of the English language and idioms we talk about sound, song, music, and/or the effects of harmonics: "I didn't like the vibes of that place (or person)"; "The pastor's words struck a chord in my mind"; "I didn't care for the tone her lecture began to take"; "That couple makes beautiful music together"; "The doctor said she is sound as a bell"; "When the cops caught him he sang like a canary"; "At his new job he will have to sing for his supper"; "How does this sound?" (when referring to something that is written.)

Music (and various forms of sound including chanting, toning, and the playing of particular instruments to induce a meditative state) has been documented as a tool for healing the body, mind, and soul of various individuals. The human body, like all of creation, is made up of molecules that vibrate. When something in us is not working in "harmony" with the rest of the organism and environment, we are said to be in "dis-harmony." In order to return the state of balanced harmony, music, is used by many as a source of healing. One reason such healing occurs through music is due to the phenomena called Entrainment, a concept by which things are brought into harmony with one another. For example, suppose you have two or more tuning forks in a room but only strike one. An amazing thing occurs. Several of the other tuning forks begin to vibrate at the same frequency as the one that was struck. Therefore, when something in the human organism is in dis-harmony, through the power of entrainment, the organism can be brought back to a healthy state of vibration through entrainment.

Music has been used for centuries in religious and spiritual rituals, but more recently, music is finding its way into many modern day therapeutic settings and hospitals. Advertisers and movie makers have long understood that music can effect the mood of a viewer. For the well crafted commercial, a consumer is much more likely to recall a product that is set to a jingle (music) than one with out.

Many deaf people do not hear the music that the interpreters are interpreting. However, if the interpreter does what I am suggesting in this text, the auditory music will become visual music and, as such, have similar benefits.

Kinesthetic therapy is also gaining greater recognition in the field of therapies and healing modalities as is drama therapy and dance therapy. Each of these take the participant, via movement, to a place where healing can occur. As interpreters (performers) we are also moving. The fact that we are engaging our kinesthetic faculties places us in a position where we can benefit from the practice of interpreting music. The manner in which we sign, move, and emote can tap into the benefits that kinesthetic, drama, and dance therapies offer. But those specific benefits do not stop with us.

Through "empathetic response" the viewer goes on the journey with us. While many of you may not be familiar with the term "empathetic response," you, in fact are familiar with what it means. Have you ever watched a movie and one of the characters stubs his or her toe or hits his or her head and YOU cringe in pain? That is empathetic response. Anytime we watch a movie or see new footage, or witness an accident and we feel some form or empathy for the people, we are experiencing empathetic response. Empathetic response is not always a negative experience related to pain. We can also feel a sense of inspiration, joy, and accomplishment when we witness an event or circumstance that elicits that feeling. We can feel a surge of emotion or harmony with the Ailey dancer as he leaps through the air, lands and assists his female partner to her feet. That is also an experience of empathetic response.

Through the manner in which we embody music, we can be a source of entrainment, a source of visual harmony that has the ability to inspire, empower, and "heal" not only the viewer but ourselves as well.

While I know this barely scratches the surface and possibly leaves you wanting more (maybe a second edition could be more in depth), my goal for including this segment was to remind you or to instill in you that signing is never just signing and that interpreting is never just interpreting. We have the capabilities of being a conduit or an instrument for amazing change and transformations to occur. . . but that starts with "YOU." You - releasing your baggage, you becoming more whole, more harmonious, more caring, and empowered. I encourage you to take up your bed and walk, for the journey of a thousand miles begins with one step!

THE CURTAIN COMES DOWN

No single text can cover all of the possible terms, techniques, tactics, skills, nuances of anything you are striving to learn. It was my intention to "wet your appetite," so to speak, by giving you enough of an introduction to this art of music and ASL that I have come to love so much. Lao Tzu said, "The journey of a thousand miles begins with one step." It was my intention that this be merely one step on your journey. For some of you, this may be your first step, and for others it may be one of a long already begun series of steps along your journey. No matter where you are along that journey, I pray you found something of benefit within these pages.

The process of performing/interpreting/translating songs as you see is not a "simple" one and that is why many people in my observation do more transliterating of songs instead of interpreting them. More people prefer the English grammar versus the more idiomatic ASL grammar. Some do so because that is what the client prefers; some do so because it is easier for them, while others do so because they don't know the other options.

However, it is also my experience that many people in both the deaf and hearing communities prefer a more idiomatic ASL, a visually and conceptually accurate portrayal of the music. I also would like to add that the challenge is well worth taking as it will increase the colors you have access to on your ASL palette. The more colors you have, the more skills you have, the better conversationalist you will be, the better interpreter you will be, and the better ASL performing artist you will be as well!

I wish you well in your journey.

RAYISMS

What is the story?

What Does It Mean?

How Do You Put It On Your Hands?

How Do You Put It On Your Body?

How are you building your palette?

Is it visually pleasing?

What does it look like?

The Rule of 3

Show Me Don't Tell Me

Get out of the box

ABOUT THE AUTHOR

Though his fascination with ASL began when he was a child, watching Linda Bove signing on Sesame Street, Ray's formal education in ASL did not begin until he was a student at Carlow College in Pittsburgh, Pennsylvania. While he was an undergraduate student at Carlow, he had the opportunity to take a class entitled - "Manual Communication." After contacting the instructor, Karen McGann – Director of the Catholic Offices for Deaf persons, she told him it was in fact an ASL class. He immediately registered.

For the entire first half of the class, he did horribly! He could not grasp the English – ASL continuum concept. He wanted to sign English but we were signing something, which at the time was called Pidgin Signed English or PSE (currently referred to as Contact Signing). It wasn't until midterms that he began to make a breakthrough and grasp the differences in the language structures. For midterms, Karen assigned the task of signing a song for the class. As he sat down and worked through the song, taking the source language of English and trying to translate that into the target gloss so he could then put it on his hands (i.e., sign it), it proved to be a most enlightening experience. It was through that task that his mind took hold of the ASL concept.

Karen also introduced him to two performing companies in Pittsburgh, and because of that meeting, she encouraged him to create his own company. From that encouragement, S.T.A.R.S. (Sticking Together Always Results in Success) A Guiding Light in the Midst of Darkness was founded first in Pittsburgh (1993), then a Richmond chapter (2001) was founded as well.

He attended all of the non-credit classes held at the Center on Deafness at the Western Pennsylvania School for the Deaf, where he later became a summer camp counselor for one year. Having taken all of the classes offered there, he continued taking non-credit courses through the Community College of Allegheny County (CCAC) and that lead to applying to the Interpreter Training Program at CCAC, under the direction of Dr. Brian Cerney. He completed the program, became an interpreter as well as a certified teacher of ASL through the ASLTA an American Sign Language Teacher's Association, continued to travel and perform with S.T.A.R.S., and then relocated to Richmond, Virginia, where he attended Virginia Commonwealth University (VCU) and received superb instruction in the theatre department, and later obtained his Master of Fine Arts in Theater Pedagogy.

Upon graduating from VCU, he was offered a job in Washington, DC, working for the Wild Zappers and the National Deaf Dance Theater under the direction of Fred Beam. Ray was the company's traveling interpreter and guest performing artist for approximately a year before he began teaching at Southeastern University, Prince George's Community College, and the Arlington Adult Education program. Teaching and freelance interpreting then consumed most of his time. His return to the theatre happened when he was offered an interpreting job. While working for The Open Circle Theater Company, as a rehearsal interpreter, during their production of "Jesus Christ Superstar", which included both Deaf and hearing actors, Ray met deaf actress, director, teacher Monique Holt. Monique Holt recommended that Ray audition for the Interpreting for the Theater Institute; which is a one-week institute held at Julliard in NYC. The institute is for proficient sign language interpreters who want to refine their skills for interpreting in the theater. Classes are taught by New York's top theatrical Broadway interpreters, as well as by deaf professionals. The Juilliard School sponsors this program with the Theater Development Fund.

Taking her advice, he contacted the program, auditioned and during the summer of 2005, attended the Julliard Theater Interpreting week long training in NYC. Under the instruction and guidance of four top-notch teachers, who are also top-notch interpreters Alan Champion and Candace Broecker-Penn, Lynnette Taylor, and Stephanie Feyne, he had a life changing experience. This life changing experience was also shared by his wonderful peers, fellow interpreters from around the country, who attended the program with Ray.

Because of all his years using ASL, being in the Deaf community, interpreting, performing, teaching, studying, and ever-evolving, Ray has realized he is not the only one who loves ASL and its beauty as a language and art form. Many people have asked him to teach workshops, tutor, and perform over the years. This book will illustrate some of what he tends to cover in those classes and sessions. He always reminds, "My method is not the way, just a possible way."

Raymont Anderson is what we commonly call a life long student. He loves the process of learning new things and improving the skills that he already possesses. After completing the thirteen years of public school (K – 12), Ray went on to obtain an Associate Degree in illustration and graphic design from the Art Institute of Pittsburgh; his Bachelor of Arts in Art Education from Carlow College, an Associate Degree in interpreting and certificate in deaf studies from Community College of Allegheny county; his Master of fine Arts in Theatre Pedagogy from Virginia Commonwealth University; his Doctor of Divinity from The American Institute of Holistic Theology. Upon completion of his D.D., Ray also became an ordained Reverend by the United Christian Fellowship. Currently at this writing, Ray is completing a dual PhD program. Through the American Institute of Holistic Theology he is completing a PhD in metaphysics and through the University of Sedona, a PhD in Holistic Life Coaching while also getting certified as a Holistic Life Coach through Spencer Institute.

While living in the DC metro area, Ray established a new American Sign Language theatrical performance company. The name of the company is B.E.L.I.E.V.E. (Being Empowered, Living Inspired, Exemplifying Victory Everyday.)

Presently, Ray is writing two inspirational, self-help books on improving your life and one fictional book about an action hero named Hikari (Japanese for "light".) He is also a Holistic Life Coach, Reiki master, and founder of The P.H.O.E.N.I.X. Institute which is in the process of becoming a facility for holistic development training for people seeking lives of empowerment, abundance, and success. Ray is also beginning to do more visual art work (drawing, painting, photography) and intends to start selling his art again and open an art gallery. He also intends to take his acting skills to TV and film where he will have his own TV show(s) and several starring roles in films. Of course the learning will not end. While he may not enroll in a degree program again, Ray will continue to take classes, attend workshops, and read voraciously. He still aspires to learn Chinese, Japanese, and Spanish; to play piano; to sing; and take formal dance classes to name a few.

Dr. Anderson is available for workshops, lectures, performances and presentations. He is also open to questions and comments about the text. Feel free to contact him regarding your inquiries and comments.

Rev. Dr. Raymont L. Anderson
www.whenyoubelieve.org
RaymontAnderson@yahoo.com
Anderson.Raymont@gmail.com
www.thephoenixinstitutetransformyourlife.org
RaymontAnderson@thephoenixinstitutetransformyourlife.org

Stay tuned for more to come . . . (smile)

References

Lentz, E. M., Mikos, K., Smith, C., & Dawn Sign Press. (1988). Signing naturally teacher's curriculum guide. San Diego, CA: DawnSign Press.

Valli, C. & Lucas, C. (2000). Linguistics of American Sign Language. (3rd ed.). Washington, DC: Gallaudet University Press.

Appendix A: Additional Resources

Books
Acting: Onstage and Off
by Robert Barton
Publisher: Wadsworth Publishing; 4 edition
ISBN-10: 0534637086

American Sign Language Green Books, A Teacher's Resource Text on Grammar and Culture (American Sign Language Series) (Paperback)
by Charlotte Baker-Shenk, Dennis Cokely
Publisher: Gallaudet University Press
ISBN-10: 093032384X

Basic Concepts in Modern Dance: A Creative Approach (Dance Horizons Book)
by Gay Cheney
Publisher: Princeton Book Company Publishers; 3 edition
ISBN-10: 0916622762

Choreography: A Basic Approach Using Improvisation
by Sandra Cerny Minton
Publisher: Human Kinetics Publishers; 3 edition
ISBN-10: 0736064761

Dance, Mind & Body
by Sandra Cerny Minton
Publisher: Human Kinetics Publishers; 1 edition
ISBN-10: 0736037896

Dance Composition: A Practical Guide to Creative Success in Dance Making
by Ja Smith-Autard
Publisher: Theatre Arts Book; 5 edition
ISBN-10: 0878301976

The Encyclopedia of Acting Techniques: Illustrated Instruction, Examples and Advice for Improving Acting Techniques and Stage Presence--From Tragedy to Comedy, Epic to Farce
by John Perry
Publisher: Betterway Books
ISBN-10: 1558704566

Idioms in the Bible Explained and A Key to the Original Gospels
by George M. Lamsa
Publisher: HarperOne
ISBN-10: 0060649275

Interpreting at Church: A Paradigm for Sign Language Interpreters
by Leo Yates Jr.
Publisher: BookSurge Publishing
ISBN-10: 1419653180

Lessons In Laughter
by Bernard Bragg, Eugene Bergman
Publisher Gallaudet University Press
ISBN-10: 0930323467

Meaning-Based Translation: A Guide to Cross-Language Equivalence, 2nd edition
by Mildred L. Larson
Publisher: University Press of America; 2 edition
ISBN-10: 0761809716

A Practical Handbook for the Actor (Paperback)
by Melissa Bruder, Lee Michael Cohn, Madeleine Olnek, Nathaniel Pollack, Robert Previtio, Scott Zigler
Publisher: Vintage; 1 edition
ISBN-10: 0394744128

A Sense of Dance: Exploring Your Movement Potential
by Constance A. Schrader
Publisher: Human Kinetics Publishers; 2nd edition
ISBN-10: 0736051899

So You Want to Be an Interpreter: An Introduction to Sign Language Interpreting
by Janice H. Humphrey, Bob Alcorn
Publisher: H & H Pub Co; 3rd edition
ISBN-10: 0964036770

Relaxation And Stress Reduction Workbook
by Martha Davis
Publisher: NEW HARBINGER PUBLICATIONS; 5 edition
ISBN-10: 1572242140

Religious Signing: The New Comprehensive Guide to All Faiths
By Elaine Costello
Publisher: Bantam Books
ISBN-10: 0553342444

Websites

ASL Pro (Resource dictionary)
http://aslpro.com

ASL University (Resource dictionary and ASL info)
http://www.lifeprint.com/asl101/

Austin Andrews (ASL Storyteller / Performer)
http://www.youtube.com/awti

Deaf Missions (Resources related to ASL and the Bible)
http://www.deafmissions.com

Manny Hernandez (ASL Storyteller / Performer / Teacher)
http://aslstorytelling.com/

Mark Mitchum (Deaf Pastor / Teacher / Performer)
http://www.markmitchumweb.com/

National Association of the Deaf (Non-profit organization designed to empower Deaf and Hard of Hearing Individuals)
www.nad.org/

Registry of Interpreters for the Deaf (National Association of Sign Language Interpreters in the US)
www. rid.org/

Sign Media, Inc. (Provider of video and text material on ASL and Deaf culture)
http://www.signmedia.com/

Trix Bruce (ASL Storyteller / Performer / Teacher)
http://www.trixbruce.com/

DVDs

American Masters:
Sweet Honey in the Rock: Raise Your Voice DVD
http://www.shoppbs.org/sm-pbs-american-masters-sweet-honey-in-the-rock-raise-your-voice--pi-2061401.html

ASL Poetry: Selected Works of Clayton Valli on DVD
English Captions, Voice-Over
Author: Clayton Valli
Length: One 105-minute DVD plus bonus features
ISBN: 0-915035-24-3
Audience: For All Audiences

Nathie: No Hand-Me-Downs
Nathie Marbury tells about her life and how being deaf saved her life.
http://www.harriscomm.com/catalog/product_info.php?products_id=18058

Check the sites of Manny Hernandez, Trix Bruce, and Mark Mitchum for their DVDs

Appendix: Additional Lyrics and Exercises

Billy Joel
"River of Dreams"

Walk in the middle of the I go walking in the, in the middle of
the….repeat 4x
In the middle of the night, I go walking in my sleep
From the mountains of faith to the river so deep

"Everybody talking bout heaven ain't goin there."
On that day, some will say, "Did we not prophesy in your name?"
and they'll say, "We drove out demons in your name." I know
some will say, "We performed many miracles in your name so many
works in your name."

"If I may, I have to tell May that in May, I may have to leave."

"While you run in to see about running for president, I'll let the car
run and warm up, especially since the cold makes my nose run; oh
be careful not to get a run in your stocking and try not to run into
chatty Cathy, she runs her mouth far too much. Darn, did I leave
the water in the bathroom running?"

APPENDIX: ADDITIONAL ILLUSTRATIONS

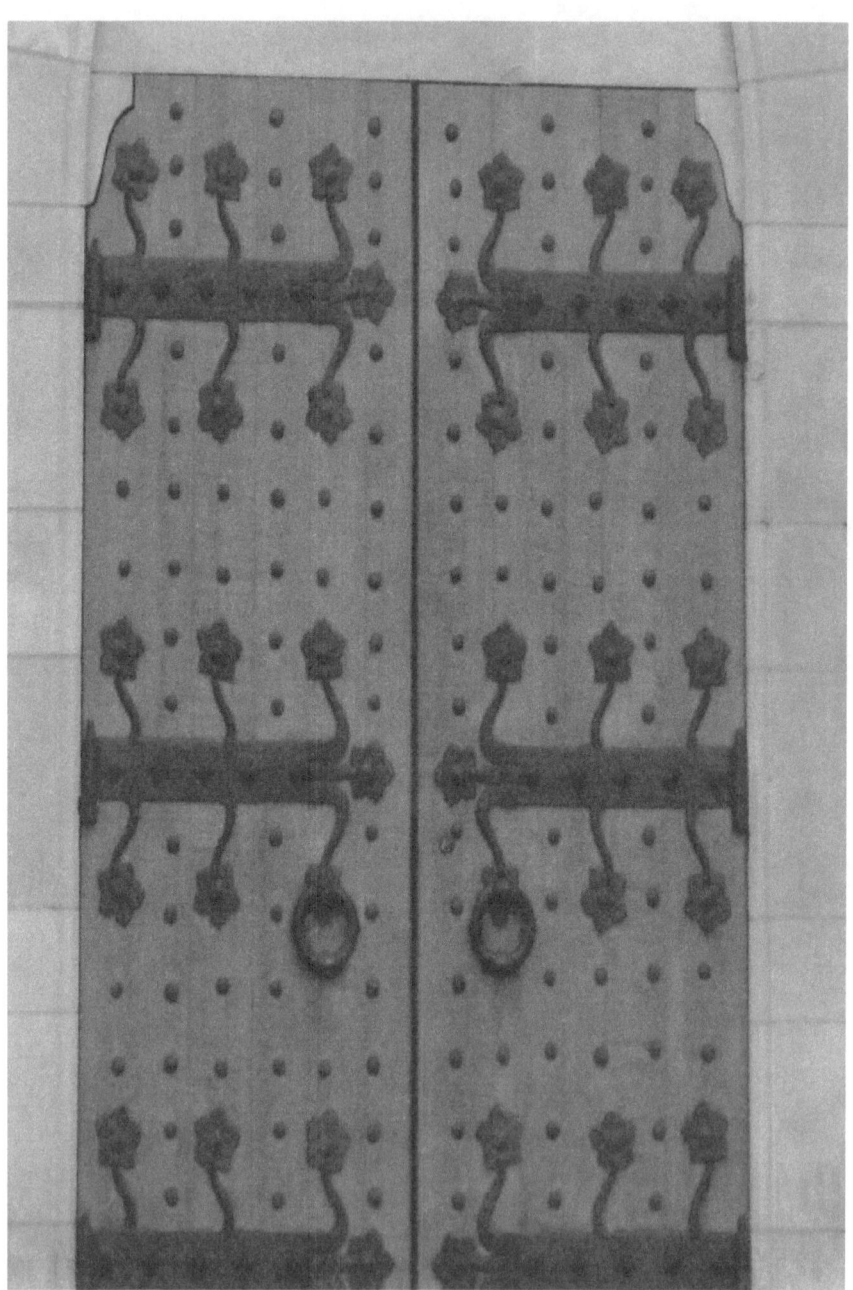

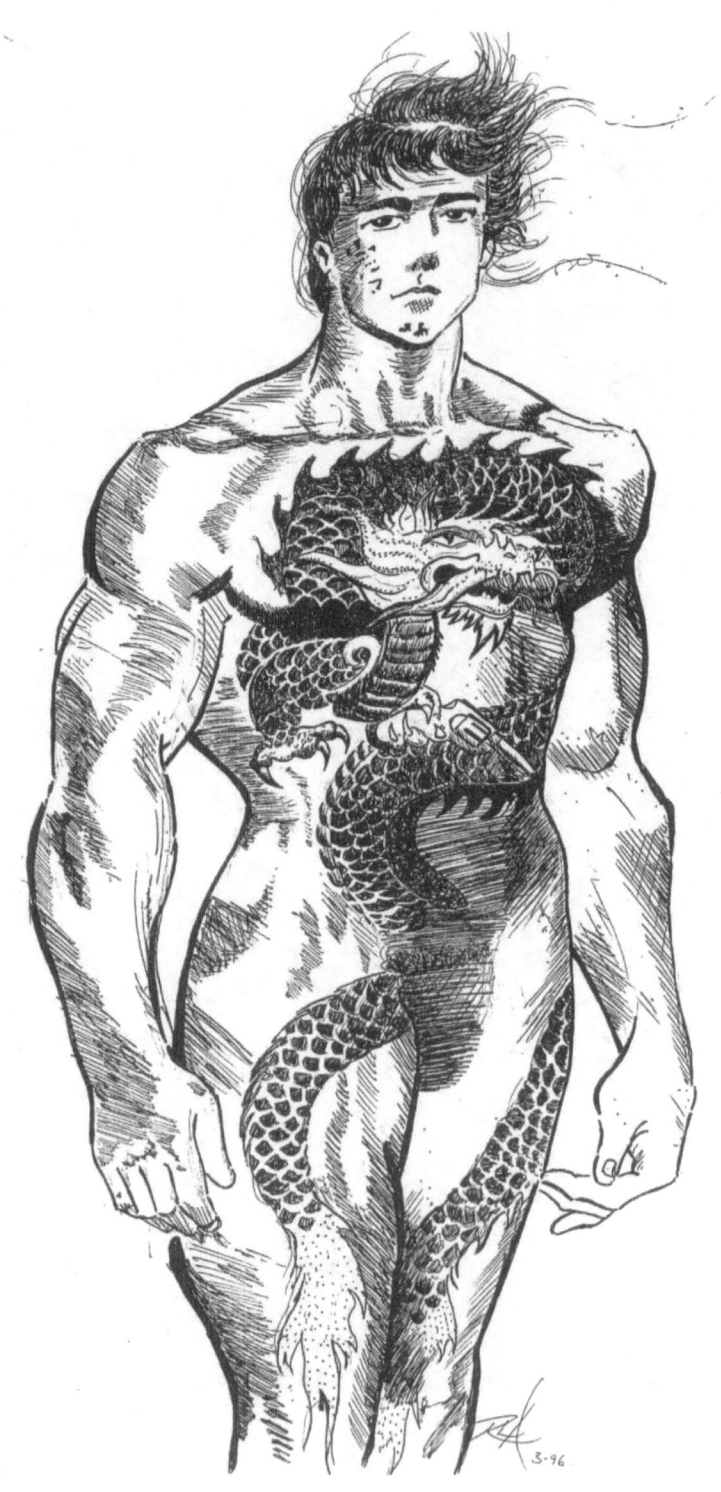